STAGE BY STAGE

To
Robert and Anna,
the future

STAGE
BY STAGE

Rallying with RUSSELL BROOKES

Russell Brookes
with Neil Perkins

MRP

MOTOR RACING PUBLICATIONS LTD
Unit 6, The Pilton Estate, 46 Pitlake, Croydon CR0 3RY, England

First Published 1991

British Library Cataloguing in Publication Data

Brookes, Russell
    Stage by stage: rallying with Russell Brookes.
    1. Cars. Rallying
    I. Title
    796.72092

ISBN 0-947981-56-X

The publishers gratefully acknowledge the assistance of all those who
supplied photographs for this book, including Martin Holmes Rallying,
LAT Photographic, Stuart McCrudden Associates, Colin Taylor
Productions and Rob Whale

Typeset by
Ryburn Typesetting Ltd, Halifax, West Yorkshire

Printed in Great Britain by
The Amadeus Press Ltd, Huddersfield, West Yorkshire

Contents

John Andrews

Introduction

I am delighted to have been invited to write the introduction to this book – although so far I have only been allowed to see the chapter headings. By way of personal background, I was first introduced to Russell Brookes by one Derek Hill in Wolverhampton in early 1974. Derek earned his corn by bringing people together – as well as writing about them – and his timing was excellent because my Wolverhampton based company, Andrews Industrial Equipment Limited, was coming up to ten years of age and we were looking for an appropriate way to mark that milestone.

I had just previously been wooed by a hot-air balloonist, whose activity was obviously appropriate, being synonymous with 'Heat for Hire' (spelt 'Hire' or 'Higher'!), but a crash landing after only a few seconds' flight created some reservations on my part.

I was, however, taken with the relative calm of Derek Hill's protege, Russell Brookes, and his obvious quiet determination and presentability. A nationwide rallying theme had relevant appeal to a young company with staff operating from strategic points around the country, and those of our people who celebrated the company's tenth anniversary at Chateau Impney near Droitwich will never forget the brief visit by Russell and his co-driver John Brown on their way to an early event – I think it was the Cheltenham Festival rally.

As readers of this book will understand, that 'sending off' was to be the start of a highly successful and enviable business/sport relationship – the current terminology is 'sports sponsorship' but I am not sure the phrase had been invented at that time. Whatever it was, it worked in many ways and we all enjoyed it – even if it did mean putting some effort into it.

I well remember getting covered in mud by guess who on my first foray as a rally spectator on the 1974 Avon Tour of Britain, and Jill, my wife, will never forget leaving the sleeping town of Lucca in Italy early one morning in 1979 to drive over a thousand miles through Italy, Switzerland and Germany into Belgium, intending to support Russell on his first Ypres 24 Hours event. We arrived somewhat saddle-sore in Ypres at midnight, to be delayed by an ambulance coming out through the hallowed Menin Gate. In the dark, we managed to find the little hotel at which Russell had been staying and had arranged accommodation for us, only to be told that the ambulance had been called out after Russell's high-speed crash caused by a jammed throttle. Fortunately neither he nor his co-driver Paul White were hurt, and all we needed was a bed. Jill and I, much to our disgust at the time, were taken off to another hotel a few miles away in the village of Lo, the owners of which could not have been more welcoming and, in subsequent years, became good friends of both the Brookes and Andrews families.

I recall being woken in the early hours of one morning by an ecstatic Russell informing me that he and John Brown had just won their first national event, the Granite City: despite the stupid time of day, I shared their delight of course.

Equally, I shall never forget my first opportunity as a co-driver, on a charity event in the Peterborough area. The hedges, the brick walls, the dykes, the spectators – all went past in a blur as my driver opposite locked our way through the stages, alternately light and heavy footed on the throttle. Now I knew how Russell managed to wear out a new pair of leather gloves during a handful of stages – and he told me afterwards that, because I was with him, he had only been driving at nine-tenths!

Through our involvement in rallying, some of the Andrews staff and my family have enjoyed the companionship of one of the sport's great characters who has proved to be extremely competent and entertaining not only behind the wheel but equally so at the dinner table and in business. My association with Russell Brookes has been good for the Andrews company, for its all-important people, and for our respective families. There can be no finer testimony to the latter aspect than the fact that Jill and I were invited to be godparents to Russell and Julia's first-born, Robert.

I am sure you will enjoy what follows. I certainly will.

John Andrews

ANDREWS•SYKES

Peter Webber

Acknowledgement

When John Blunsden of Motor Racing Publications drew up the first synopsis for this book, it had a chapter entitled 'The Andrews Years' but it was not intended that it should be principally biographical. As the first sections were written, however, it became clear that you could hardly separate the rest of my rally career from the story of the Andrews association, for as far as we know it is the longest active continuous sponsorship in motorsport, dating back as it does to the Donegal Rally in June 1974.

The RAC Rally organizers claim their deal with Lombard was signed earlier than our own, but their names did not appear together in public until November that year. No doubt someone will find a trade sponsorship that has lasted longer but I think we can legitimately claim our association to be special. So this is where my acknowledgment starts, for Andrews have enabled me to stay active in rallying, winning events, for 17 years, and to make a career out of my sport.

I remember very clearly my first meeting with John Andrews and Eric Johnson at which the proposal was put forward. I must acknowledge Derek Hill for making that introduction which brought me not only motorsport sponsorship but friendship from John and Jill Andrews and their whole family; their children (now grown up) Richard, Juliet and Philip and their families, and John and Jill's parents. Julia and I are pleased we are now part of that family, as John and Jill are godparents to our son Robert. Special thanks are due to Eric Johnson for making that first plunge into motorsport possible. Within Andrews, my closest links have been with the Advertising and Marketing Department which for two long periods was headed by David Cooper, who was always unfailingly enthusiastic, and likewise Rod Lloyd, who also put the nuts and bolts of the publicity together so well and has been so supportive over the years.

As the company changed from Andrews to Andrews Sykes, Andrew Fitton, Chief Executive of the Braithwaite Group, created an exciting year in 1989 and introduced the new Managing Director, Peter Webber. Peter is really a football man at heart but recognizes that special association, and I wish to thank him for personal support during a period of change, and for making this book possible.

This is also my opportunity to say thank you to all those directors and staff, past and present, who have helped make Andrews Sykes a very successful company of which I am glad to have been a part, and which will have a great future.

Acknowledgement must also be given to Keith and Mike Hill of Brooklyn Garages whose sponsorship came before the Andrews connection. Going back further, special thanks to the mechanics, friends from Land Rover, members of Redditch Car Club and so many others who gave freely of their services on rallies in the days before sponsorship and factory contracts. A special mention is due of 'my mate' Allen Goodall who, after every rally it sometimes seemed, put the bodywork back together again.

Of my many rallying crew-members, I must mention John Brown and Neil Wilson, who have been wise counsellors and given so much more than just a co-driver's help.

Looking beyond motorsport, I would like to say thanks to Andrew Smith, whose brainchild was Russell Brookes Print Ltd, in which we are partners: it has had much success and shows even more promise for the future.

I found the thought of writing a book daunting, and the task has been made far easier by the great effort and patience of Neil Perkins, who has made sense out of tape recordings, researched the facts, typed the text, and given form to the chapters. Thanks also to editor John Plummer, and John Blunsden of MRP for his flexible deadlines and his concept of the way the book should look.

Finally and most important of all, my wife Julia, who said, 'I want an acknowledgement, a dedication sounds too final.' Marriages and motorsport are notoriously bad companions, but throughout the separations she has kept a great home, brought up two fine children, and maintained a reasonably even keel when every December 31 I was technically out of work. Without her love and support it would not have been possible.

Russell Brookes
Besford, Worcester
December 1990

Working at the weekends

1

Looking back at my early life, it wasn't immediately obvious that I should become interested in motorsport. I was the only son of a leading fireman, who spent his time after the war setting up a building and plastering company in the King's Heath area of Birmingham. I was born on August 16, 1945, VJ Day, at Selly Oak Hospital. The running joke in the family was that the Americans had dropped the second atomic bomb and I was the result!

I grew up with the family in a semi-detached house in Lindsworth Road, King's Norton. Although I was an only child, it certainly wasn't a solitary childhood because many other youngsters lived in the area and I made numerous friends. Indeed, some of the friendships from that part of my life have stayed true ever since. My earliest contact was Chris Wright, who lived three doors away. He was later to be the best man at my wedding and he is somebody with whom I still keep in close contact. Another friend was Roger Clements, living two doors away, who eventually joined the Royal Air Force following a time at Jaguar where he completed his engineering training. I still see Roger frequently; he has now become a Wing Commander, formerly of a squadron of Phantoms and more recently of a ground-to-air missile unit.

We moved house when I was ten years old and went to live in King's Heath. Though it was only three miles from where I spent my earliest days, it was a dramatic move for me, in that it severed my links with close friends at a time when I changed school too. This was a lonely period and I didn't make many friends in the new neighbourhood.

I wasn't a keen pupil and I must confess that I didn't enjoy my time at school. I passed my 11-plus examination and went to King Edward's Grammar School, Camp Hill, in Birmingham. I did manage to pass O-levels, but although I achieved good marks in both history and geography, I was directed for some reason or another – I suspect because of my father's building interests – towards

mathematics, physics and chemistry. He had wanted me to become a civil engineer. I stayed on for three years in the sixth form at King Edward's and failed all the A-levels miserably. So really, I look back on my time at school as being rather a waste, especially as my sporting prowess was somewhat less impressive than my academic achievements!

I learnt to drive a car at about the age of 12 when I took my father's A70 Hereford out on Shenstone airfield. Of course it wasn't for some time that I got an opportunity to drive myself on public roads. I was interested in racing and we went to quite a few motor races, particularly vintage car events and a number of Grand Prix meetings. I think my favourite machine at that time was the short-lived single-seater Aston Martin, the end of the era of front-engined Formula 1 cars.

I eventually took my driving test on December 15, 1962 and almost immediately after passing I entered my first motorsport event, which was a production car trial. I borrowed my mother's Renault Dauphine and did a Dudley & District Car Club event, which took place on the 'Tocky Bonk' behind Fred Corbett's garage in Brierley Hill. To my surprise, I actually won the class. There were four people in the car, including two very big friends, Chris Wright and Roger Clements, who sat in the back seat acting as bouncers. The first three places overall were taken by Volkswagens, but as they weren't eligible for class positions I finished first in the section. It was a fairly auspicious start, to say the least.

I'd joined a local club, the Hagley & District Car Club, which met at Perry Hall in Bromsgrove, and it was going down to their meetings which started me off on the rally trail. As with most clubs of its type, everything seemed to revolve around the bar and drinking – of course, that was in the days before the breathalyser! It was there that I met David Southwell, who told me all about the intricacies of night rallying and what fun it was. He described very

A young Russell Brookes consults Father Christmas.

graphically and very excitedly how you tore down the country lanes in the middle of the night and visited controls, keeping to a strict time schedule. He persuaded me to enter an event, the Birmingham University Mermaid Rally, and told me that I should do the driving. 'I'll do the navigating and we'll use your car,' he said. It was then that things started to go wrong.

The event took place in heavy snow in the March of 1963, which people remember as being one of the worst winters this century. I originally planned to enter a Mini which my father had bought for me. It had been slightly modified and was purchased with the intention of doing some hillclimbs and sprints. Then my father borrowed the car, skidded on some ice and damaged it the weekend before the rally. He felt sorry for me and said I could use his Austin Westminster. Neither of us really knew what rallying was about at this point: I think we both thought in terms of a regularity event where you had to keep to a 30mph average speed.

The only concession to competition use was that the Austin had adjustable shock absorbers, fitted for towing the family caravan. It was powered by a hefty 2.6-litre six-cylinder engine. The roads by now had been snowploughed but were still covered in snow. A fairly big, heavy car was quite good in the conditions and I discovered that we were in third place overall by the time we got to the half-way halt. This went to my head as we commenced the second half of the rally. I started to develop a new technique for getting around corners. That was to approach fairly fast and put your foot on the brakes so all the wheels locked up on the ice. You then reached under the dashboard and pulled on the umbrella handbrake. As you took your foot off the footbrake the front wheels would start to turn and grip and pull the nose of the car in towards the corner. It was then a big panic to release the handbrake before the tail slid out too far.

Inevitably, on one occasion I missed the handbrake! The car spun in the road and slid quite slowly sideways down a hill on the ice. Unfortunately, a farmer had dug his way out of an adjoining field: the car pivoted on the pile of snow that remained and rolled gently three or four times down the road.

The Austin was still drivable, although it had no glass intact. It was one of the coldest drives I've ever had in my life as we made our way home. I remember arriving at the top of our road, switching off the engine and coasting the last quarter of a mile into our front drive. I pushed the car into the garage and then sat in it for the rest of the night wondering whether I should wake my father and tell him immediately, or whether I should let him have a good night's sleep first. Eventually I decided on the latter course, but it didn't make much difference. He was mad! The insurance company wouldn't pay out because the car had been damaged in a rally and my father sold my Mini to finance repairs to the Austin. At this point my early rally career came to a premature end.

I had a group of friends all interested in motorsport, particularly in rallying, but it was not an enthusiasm which had any direction to it and, as far as I was concerned, there was certainly no ambition to become a works driver at that time. Amongst our group, Roger Platt was always considered to be the one who would make it as a driver, not me, and I spent two years navigating for Roger on many events. Also around at that time was Allen Goodall, who set up a company called Goodbrook Motors in partnership with myself for about a year, and he was significant later on in terms of helping me with the preparation of cars. Another friend on the scene was Jasper Carrott, and we spent much of the time tearing around the local lanes in Minis, or whatever we could get our hands on. In fact, Jasper wrote a song about my car which he sang at his folk club in Solihull, The Boggery: it began –

'If you ever see me standing in a stupor
You'll know that Russell's come and brought his Mini-
    Cooper . . .'

He claims to have forgotten the rest of the lyric, and I can't say I blame him – hardly vintage stuff, but it was early days!

The great annual outing for us all was a Whitsun trip to St Ives in Cornwall. Getting back home to Birmingham afterwards tended to become something of a race. I took the unofficial record in an Austin-Healey 100M, completing the trip in four hours, twenty minutes – not bad in the days before motorways. Roger Platt was not far behind in an old A55 Cambridge. Eventually we all formed the Girt Clog Climbing Club – more to do with drinking than climbing – and we meet in the Lake District for the Annual General Meeting. The club draws together all the people I knew from that era, from all over the place, and awards such as the 'Golden Boot', for the one who has made the greatest effort to get there, are given.

Like many people at that sort of age I really didn't have a plan for my career, and life took a number of twists and turns, particularly when my father died. The surviving plastering company was left to my mother and myself, although the building business and other activities were put into receivership. I was trained as a quantity surveyor with R M Douglas, a major civil engineering company. I left there because they insisted we worked on Saturdays and I wasn't prepared to do that, it intruded too much into my private life and into my motorsport.

I joined my father's plastering company which prospered and was particularly successful in Birmingham during the building boom of the 1960s. We gradually moved away from plastering into an area of specialist finishing which was undertaken on a sub-contract basis for a company in Highbridge, Somerset. They, in turn, had won the contract to do all the underpasses and blocks of flats in Birmingham – a contract specifically placed with them by the City Architect, Maudslay. The process was intended to cover up the shuttering marks in concrete: any spraying process only highlighted what was underneath, and hence they called in a firm of plasterers to apply a surface covering. It was a time of increasing prosperity, with a lot of profitable work going on.

Then it all collapsed when Maudslay was convicted of fraud with the city's money. After an investigation of the contracts that he had placed, the whole thing came to a complete grinding halt and I was left with nothing but a residue of ten tons of coloured granite granules, the principal material which had been involved in the surfacing process!

It was then that I set up a business with Jasper Carrott. We decided to produce and sell decorative lamp bases made out of Mateus Rosé and VAT 69 bottles: we added a light fitting, covered them with glue and sprayed them with these coloured granite granules. Jasper had an outlet for them at that time as he was selling off a barrow at various markets in the Black Country. We found someone who could obtain the bottles for us and established a little production line.

We produced hundreds of those little lamps. Sales were very brisk for the first week, as Jasper did a different market every day, but when he went back to Dudley he virtually got lynched because we'd missed off the vital finishing touch – a piece of green baize on the bottom! People took these decorative lamps home and the coloured granite granules scratched hell out of their mantelpieces and sideboards. We had to take them all

back, often in bits as Jasper ducked and weaved to miss the flying bottles.

So the business had to be closed down and I joined Land Rover, where I worked in the lowest of low jobs for a time as a technical correspondent. I actually enjoyed myself at the company and remained there until 1977 when I got my first works-contracted drive, eventually becoming an assistant manager in Product Planning. It was a wide-ranging job that included co-ordinating the building of special vehicles, from the King of Nepal's armoured coronation Land Rover to 6,000 units for the Moroccan Police. The other half of the department bought and road tested competitors' vehicles, so it had a close association with engineering and production. This gave me the opportunity to acquire useful knowledge later applicable in the area of rally car development.

Motorsport was still only a hobby at this time. After buying another Mini 850 which was successfully campaigned in hillclimbs and sprints, including holding quite a few class records, I eventually saved up enough money to buy an Austin-Healey 100M. I didn't use that in competition, though, because it would never have been reliable enough. I spent my time navigating for friends on rallies instead, and for quite a few years co-drove in a Borgward Isabella Estate – not the most likely of rallying vehicles.

Then I bought an Austin-Healey Sprite for £72, intending to go motor racing. It was stripped down, a glassfibre body was added and I installed an old Formula 3 BMC engine. It never really worked, and retired in every race I entered – the engine either blew up or overheated. It was most unsuccessful.

One of the most memorable experiences was acting as service crew on the RAC and Welsh International rallies for Richard Hudson-Evans, then a Lucas Engineering apprentice. This was at a time when the RAC was a rally with three days and two nights out of bed at a stretch, and that was only the first half of the event! On the Welsh,

The first Mini 850 used in local hillclimbs and sprints.

Installing a BMC Formula 3 engine in this Austin-Healey Sprite seemed like a good idea for circuit racing but brought nothing more than expensive mechanical failures.

I went out with Roger Platt. Servicing then was a haphazard affair, and we met Richard whenever we could on the side of the road. Trying to be clever, we spotted what looked like an ideal opportunity to service between two night stages which I now know to be Epynt. After driving up the narrow lanes and seeing no marshals we set up at what seemed a likely spot and put out the 'service' board. The first car through in a wild opposite-lock slide was Toney Cox in a works Rover 2000. 'Wow! That was a bit fast for public roads,' said Roger. After half a dozen more cars had passed it slowly dawned on us that we were servicing on a stage. Richard arrived, slowed down – no doubt confused – accelerated, slowed down again and then disappeared into the mist in a cloud of oil smoke, annoyed at losing valuable time.

Roger Platt and I then decided to go for something bigger and planned to tackle the 1968 Gulf London Rally. I had intended to take part in a Mini, but was forced to cancel my entry because I couldn't prepare the car in time, so I settled for going as navigator for Roger. Although we didn't finish the event I suddenly realized how exciting it was to drive rally cars fast in the forests and what a great sport international rallying could be. That was really when my rally career began to take some direction.

I decided to finish the 850 Mini that I was building and entered it on the RAC Rally in 1968. I didn't get to the finish, but I was at one time leading the class and I found it very exciting. My co-driver for the RAC was found by placing an advert in *Motoring News*: lo and behold the man who replied was Alex Jardine, who had made a name for himself by winning one of Stuart Turner's repeated competitions held to find a driver or co-driver. Alex had gone on the Monte Carlo Rally that year with Ford as their blue-eyed boy, but he didn't hit it off too well with Jim Porter and the Ford hierarchy, so that project came to a sudden and premature stop. Alex's experience was useful, but he was petrified of a car catching fire. The Mini did just that in the middle of the Camberley stage.

I stopped and rushed around to try and extinguish the fire in the boot. I then lost another five minutes trying to find the co-driver who had run off into the trees. The car eventually came to a stop when the gear selector mechanism broke. But I was now certain that what I wanted to do was to contest international rallies.

The same 850 Mini was pressed into service again the following year, initially on the Welsh International Rally where I won my class and finished in the top 30. My co-driver this time was Alan Christopher, another respondent to an advert in *Motoring News*. We did a number of quite successful events together, although the first one had a bit of a peculiar start. When Alan arrived he was suffering from violent toothache. He took some pills to cure the pain, but these made him carsick and he then had to buy some more pills to cure the sickness. These made him drowsy so he took some 'wakey-wakey' pills – which gave him toothache again. With all those pills inside, he rattled like a pair of maracas going through the stages!

We went on to do the Scottish Rally, where we finished last overall but third in the 850cc class. On that event we had a whole series of problems with the hydrolastic units on the Mini. It was after we had decided to retire and were sitting by the side of a loch having a sandwich that we read the regulations. They stated that you could miss stages without being excluded and we worked out that if we bypassed the next ten tests we would rejoin the rally route on time, so we eventually arrived at the Dumfries time control still in the event.

Later, we remembered the reputation of the Culbin special stage in the north of Scotland. Lots of people had told us that Minis wouldn't be able to get through because of the severity of the ruts, so we decided to give that test a miss too. Six of the remaining Minis in the class went into the special stage and never came out. That's how we came to be third in class!

I then tackled the snowy 1969 RAC Rally in the same protesting Mini. We had a terrific run, eventually

Part of Russell's responsibility at Land Rover was co-ordinating the building of special vehicles like this one for the King of Nepal's Coronation.

climbing up to 15th overall before I slid off the road and threw it all away. We finished the rally though, and got quite a few mentions in the motoring papers for this performance in an 850cc car which, even by the standards of those days, was incredibly slow with only 48 or 50 horsepower in its modified form.

In 1969 I actually made a profit from my rallying exploits with the bonus monies paid out by manufacturers. This fact attracted the attention of the Inland Revenue. Although they couldn't see that there were costs involved in rallying, they were quick to see when a profit had been made. By the end of the year I was forced into a situation where I had to set up a company to handle rallying finances, and losses on rallying for the next three years could be offset against my first income. It went some way towards covering the cost of the sport.

But this was a fairly traumatic time for me, as my parents' business had to be closed down. Bank overdrafts had been secured against our house and eventually the bank repossessed the building. Fortunately I had accumulated in the region of £550 as well as a Mini van, and my mother owned a Volkswagen 1200 Beetle, but we were forced to move outside Birmingham to find a house cheap enough to afford. It was then that I bought the first home of my own, the Forge House in Inkberrow, a village some 25 miles south of Birmingham, in Worcestershire. The £550 was just sufficient to pay the deposit on the property and I lived there until 1982, before moving to Besford. Although it was a small house, my mother had nowhere else to live and had to move in with me, which rather stultified my social life. I was also joined by a maiden aunt who was very reminiscent of Margaret Rutherford and was known to all my acquaintances and rally contacts as 'Auntie'. She steadfastly refused to be known by any other name.

I decided to continue with the Mini the following year and increase its performance, now that I had the rally bug. So the 850 bodyshell now became a 998 Cooper

Group 1 and the first event was the Circuit of Ireland Rally with Gerry Wynn. This came to an ignominious end when I tried to push the car too hard over Sally Gap and ended up in a ditch.

We then did the Welsh International Rally, where I finished 18th overall, winning the Group 1 up-to-1000cc class. It was a significant result, because people paid a fair amount of attention to class wins then. Skoda were contesting the smaller-capacity classes and seemed a little concerned about the performances of my Mini on that event. I placed an entry for the Scottish Rally, without much intention of competing, but Skoda contacted me and offered a drive. It was to be my first opportunity to drive a 'works' car.

The car in question was a 1000MB, and what a heap it turned out to be! Shortly after leaving the start line it began to overheat, it blew a head gasket, and the dynamo wouldn't charge because the adjustment was faulty and it was impossible to tighten the belt. The overheating became worse and burnt a hole in a piston. We managed to coax the car along after fitting some two-stroke plugs acquired from an agricultural dealer. The car was consuming about a gallon of oil every eight miles and eventually came to a halt on the side of the A74. All there was to be done was to ring up the Czechoslovakian importers in London and tell them where their car was and go off and spectate on the event. Skoda became quite adept at scoring class wins in later years, but they still had a lot to learn in 1970. Here ended the first works drive.

I had always wanted to contest a foreign event and the Sherry Rally had been announced for later that year, with substantial sponsorship from the Sherry 'Shippers' Association. Again an advert was placed in *Motoring News* and my co-driver on this occasion was to be Peter Oddie from Carlisle. He has remained a friend and contact ever since and is still involved with the organization of the Tour of Cumbria Rally. We were as green as green could be when we tackled this event in the same Mini, now

Russell's earliest overseas event was the Sherry Rally which he contested in 1970 and 1971. This is the second of those occasions, with co-driver Kevin Gormley and the Mini in 1275 Group 2 trim, and it brought a class win and seventh overall.

The Forge House, in Inkberrow, Worcestershire, was home from 1969 until 1982.

ALX 501B took Russell as high as 15th overall on the RAC Rally in 1969 before he slid off the road and out of contention.

A class-winning performance in the Mini on the 1970 Welsh Rally attracted attention and was one of the reasons Russell was offered a works drive with Skoda.

The Skoda works drive came on the 1970 Scottish Rally, but the 1000MB turned out to be one of the worst cars Russell has ever driven.

It was back to the trusty Mini for an unsuccessful outing on the 1970 RAC International Rally of Great Britain.

sporting a 1275S Group 1 engine. The rally started in Madrid and was really just one long party from start to finish. We were introduced to Juan Carlos, who was then the pretender to the throne, with Franco still in power, and that was followed by a very large reception at the RACE headquarters at Jarama. The participants were then pushed straight out of the building, some of them stone drunk, on to the first stage which was three laps of the Jarama circuit in the opposite direction to the usual one – most competitors seemed to want to tackle it backwards, too! Adding to the confusion was the fact that the organizers had made up the entry with taxis to meet the numbers required for the European Championship. The drivers were paid the meter reading to make the trip out from Madrid to Jarama, in addition to the distance they covered going around the circuit. Apart from the taxi drivers, I remember the wife of the owner of the Jarama circuit in her MGB, stuffing the car head-on into the armco on the first corner!

The event took in a leisurely route (made more

Russell teamed up with Martin Holmes in 1971 and tackled rounds of the *Motoring News* Championship with the Mini in 1275 Group 2 form. Note the jacket and tie worn by the driver on the Semperit Welsh Marches Rally!

exciting as it was my first attempt at pace notes) through the length of Spain, to arrive at Jerez in time for the opening of the Sherry Festival. The poor protesting rally cars had to follow in convoy behind the bands and floats, overheating as they were reduced to a mere walking pace. But we had a great time on the rally, eventually finishing 10th overall and first in Group 1. There was only one other finisher in our class, a Spaniard in a Renault R5, and it was then that our problems started. The organizers found some spurious reason to disqualify us. Being so green, I didn't know how to lodge a protest or handle the situation: if I had known that a foreign competitor always has the upper hand and the right to appeal, ultimately to

FISA in Paris, and therefore can put a stop on the results, we wouldn't have been disqualified.

It had a fortunate outcome in the long term, though, in that the Sherry organization, upset by the way the problem had been handled, paid everything for us to go back and do the event again in the subsequent year, when I finished seventh overall and won the Group 2 category.

1971 started out with a more ambitious programme. Martin Holmes, well known as a rally journalist even in those days, had approached me and said that he thought I had some talent and needed some sponsorship. He considered that I needed managing and pushing in the right direction. With support from Goodyear Tyres and

19

Roadside repairs: fitting a new steering arm during the RAC Rally. It was a job which became a regular chore, all the spares being used in the course of the event.

Withers of Winsford we embarked on the *Motoring News* Rally Championship, again in the same poor old Mini, now in 1275 Group 2 form.

We had a variety of results, nothing spectacular, but all the time I was learning more about the sport. I must admit that I didn't find road rallying as exciting as driving on special stages, and although I was very much involved in road events for the next few years and it provided a lot of fun, it didn't appear to me to be the ultimate driver sport. It was very much a co-driver orientated pastime. I also came to realize just how expensive the sport could be, and eventually my season came to a stop around August time. All the money had run out, and the wear and tear on the car was phenomenal.

I decided to contest just one more event, the RAC Rally, but that was almost a disaster from the word go. The car was now in a very poor state of repair and needed a good deal of welding, again courtesy of Goodbrook Motors. I had some sponsorship from a local engine preparation firm and my engine had been sent to them for a rebuild, free of charge, but the receiver was called in and impounded my engine as well. In fact, I never saw it again. There I was, five days before the RAC Rally, without an engine for my car.

Out of desperation, I telephoned Basil Wales at British Leyland Special Tuning. They had ceased competition earlier that year, prior to the Sherry Rally, an event that they had originally intended to contest. I was told that the last works Mini engine ever built was sitting in the corner of the press garage, although the gearbox was broken and might have damaged the engine. If I cared to venture

RGG 762G, pictured on the 1972 Scottish, was acquired for £100, underwent £60-worth of preparation, and was subsequently sold for £325 on the strength of its performance on the rally – not a bad profit!

down I was to be allowed to borrow the unit, so four days before the rally I went to Abingdon and picked up this 1293 Cooper S engine, with a crossflow head and four Amal carburettors. It was exotic stuff indeed, and turned out 117bhp. After a lot of work it was discovered that the unit would not mate directly to my gearbox. Numerous modifications were undertaken, components were machined at very short notice and the engine was eventually shoehorned into the car. We had worked for two days and three nights: it was hardly the ideal preparation for the RAC Rally – or perhaps it was, for an RAC Rally in those days!

My co-driver on the event was Ian Cooper, whose brother Rod was better known in motorsport through his Speed-Sport company. He was a tower of strength throughout the event and took a lot of the load off my shoulders. He allowed me to sleep wherever possible and altogether did a magnificent job. Without him I don't think that we would have finished, and it was an event which turned out to have some fairly important consequences.

To me the fun in rallying was driving as quickly as possible and, despite having this very old, battered Mini, we put up some fastest times overall on that rally, even though it marked the first appearance of the BDA Escorts in the hands of Timo Mäkinen and people of his calibre.

That alone attracted attention, although I must admit that in between the fastest times, we had a fair number of crashes as well – something like 14 on the one event – and we eventually finished 88th overall. I have a sneaking feeling that the RAC turned a blind eye to some of the time cards where I suspect we were well over the maximum time-limit.

That was the end of that, really, as far as my rallying was concerned. The only thing left to do was to attend a rally forum organized by British Leyland where, to my surprise, the car turned out to be the star attraction. On the panel were myself, Brian Culcheth and Pat Ryan among others, and behind the curtain was the works Marina (which had won its class) and my Mini, now in an incredibly battered state. For instance, a left-hand steering arm was mounted upside down on the right-hand side because we had broken so many and run out of spares. It was all far more interesting than a pristine Marina!

The engine was duly returned to British Leyland, but the car was at the end of its life and had literally to be thrown away. The money had expired and I gave up rallying. I turned my back on motorsport to such an extent that I didn't even take the motoring papers any longer and I was quite unaware of the announcement by Ford of the Ford Escort Mexico Championship in 1972.

That turned out to be something very important indeed in my career.

Ford, having won the 1970 London–Mexico World Cup event with Hannu Mikkola, decided to make the most of that success by introducing the Escort Mexico. It was a light car powered by a 1,600cc pushrod unit, a large engine compared to those in other small cars of its day. They hit upon the idea of a one-make championship for machines with only limited modifications. The series was to take in numerous events throughout the country and was organized around a fairly complex scoring system. The most important attractions were the awards on offer at the end of the season: in the first year there were to be works drives on the Acropolis, Scottish and Welsh rallies for the drivers finishing first, second and third respectively.

Unbeknown to me, my local Ford dealers in Inkberrow had decided to enter the championship. Brooklyn Motors was run by Keith and Mike Hill and they were both keen on motorsport. I had come into contact with them before,

having borrowed their facilities many times to prepare my Minis in the earlier years. But it was a great surprise when, one night in January, there was a knock on my door from Mike Hill, who stood there and told me that Ford had started the Mexico Championship. He explained that Brooklyn wanted to be involved, and that they had been out on the RAC Rally the previous year and had – I think by chance – been standing on each of the stages where I had set the fastest times overall. Mike Hill told me how impressed they had been with my speed and driving ability, and outlined how he was willing to make available a car and all the parts, and cover the cost of doing the events, should I be interested in driving a Mexico. I had to think about it long and hard for all of two seconds before saying yes!

The only catch was that I would have to do all the preparation work myself. That wasn't unreasonable under the circumstances, but I did 32 rallies in the first year so it soon became a major task. Effectively, that year of preparation, working late into the night every weekend

With support from Brooklyn Garages, Russell and co-driver John Brown finished fourth in the first year of the Mexico series. Their car is pictured here on the 1972 *Hereford Evening News* Rally.

This shot was taken on the Boucles de Spa in Belgium when it was run as a road rally. AMJ 1L was hired for the one event, which Russell tackled with John Brown.

and most weekdays, put me off working on cars for life.

The other turn-up for that year was John Brown. The doyen of navigators had moved from York to the Midlands to become director of the Heart of England Tourist Board. He rang up within a week of Mike Hill's visit, expressing his wish to co-drive for me during the coming year. I explained about the Mexico Championship and it all fitted together well.

In 1972, we made the mistake of contesting too many events, as I feel we did in the following year too. I competed not only in the Mexico Championship, but also in the *Motoring News* series, mainly because it was John's understandable ambition to win the latter again. Coupled with the fact that I did all the home internationals in an ex-works Mini as well, this stretched resources a great deal. The Mini was provided by Tom Seal, but it was a big disaster because the driveshafts weren't up to much: if we didn't retire after an accident, a broken driveshaft let us

down. It was a common failing with the Mini.

The end result was that we finished fourth in the Mexico Championship and just outside the prizes, but Brooklyn Garage were pleased with the publicity and the work that we had put in to the programme during the year. They therefore took the plunge to continue with the Mexico Championship in 1973, and for the very first time I had a full-time mechanic. Tony Hunt, who I knew did very good preparation work and who had been out with me on a number of rallies, was employed by Brooklyn Garages and he was to do all the work on my Mexico.

I feel that the Mexico Championship was a major turning point for a lot of people, because for the first time it was possible to compete against other drivers on an equal basis. It was an effective way of assessing driving ability, and you had a car which was inherently very reliable and hence cheap to run. In the first year, when I did the 27 rallies in the Mexico, I think it cost Brooklyn

Mike Hill (centre) and Russell (fourth from left) are pictured with members of the Brooklyn team outside their Redditch premises in 1973. The rally-prepared Brooklyn Mexico was offered for an all-inclusive price of £1,565: typical advert, right, is from *Cars and Car Conversions*, June 1973.

Garages in the region of £1,500 which, even allowing for inflation, was very cheap. Because of that you were able to do lots of events and gain lots of experience. That was the great thing about the series. I wouldn't say that it brought out any new drivers, but it certainly gave existing ones a chance to shine, competitors like Will Sparrow, Tony Pond, Andy Dawson, George Hill, Nigel Rockey and myself.

In addition to contesting the 1973 Mexico series, we decided to help Brooklyn Garages capitalize on the popularity of the Mexico rally car. John Brown came up with the idea of selling the 'Brooklyn Mexico': the garage took a brand new car, put all the bits that weren't used in competition back in the stores and built up a replica of our rally car. It was an immense success, because not only did it give the garage publicity, it increased sales as well. I believe Brooklyn sold 14 replicas which were '£1,565 on the road, including car tax.' It was cheap rallying.

1973 was a very significant year, because although the outcome in terms of results didn't lead straight to greater things at that stage, it was important for my appreciation of my own abilities. At the end of 1972 I had won my first event, the Taunton Rally, a round of the Mexico Championship, and after winning that one rally anything other than winning didn't seem to matter any more. That was the real objective. It wasn't just to go faster than other people or just to have fun, which is what rallying had been up until then. It became clear to me that winning actually mattered and was important to me personally.

For his second Mexico Championship prize drive, Russell persuaded Ford to let him tackle the 1973 RAC Rally. This shot of the ATV *Today*-**backed car was taken one or two corners before it rolled out of the event in Sutton Park!**

The new season started off very well with a win on the Targa Rusticana, with Derek Tucker co-driving because John Brown was the organizer of the event. The championship that year was divided into quarterly awards, as well as a major overall prize of a loaned works car, together with all the parts and sponsorship to run it for a season. That must be one of the best prizes offered to any rally driver ever. The winner of each quarter of the year had two drives in British Championship events in a works car as part of the full factory team.

I was very pleased to win the first quarterly award. For various reasons I wasn't able to drive the works car at a test session, but I tackled the Jim Clark Rally all the same. Therefore, when I left the start ramp in Duns the car was all very new and very strange. I had never sat in anything

faster than a Group 1 Mexico before, and here I was in a 245bhp, 2-litre works BDA Escort, entered on a round of the British Championship. All the regular contenders of the day were present, Will Sparrow, Paul Faulkner, Andrew Cowan, Mike Hibbert and people of that ilk, together with Roger Clark. I must admit that I felt very overawed by the circumstances.

Nevertheless, we had several fastest stage times. I did roll the car, luckily without too much damage and without losing too much time, and we finished second overall to Roger. Arguably, without the roll we could have won the event. That was very significant to me, because for the first time I had got into a proper factory car and realized how much faster they travelled and how much better they were than anything that I had driven before.

I also realized that I had the capability of driving these cars, and driving them as fast as or faster than anyone else. From that moment I developed the ambition to become a works rally driver: it wasn't until then that the idea had been planted in my mind.

Strangely, the result had little significance to other people. Because of clashes in the calendar, the rally attracted only minimal publicity and Ford weren't keen to make a lot of it because it occurred at a time when the company was having a major cut-back in its competition activities. I think that the thought of another young driver coming along rather horrified them as it would have stretched their resources to an even greater extent.

For the second Mexico Championship prize drive we persuaded Ford to let me compete on the RAC Rally. The event finished disastrously as I rolled out on the fourth test, Sutton Park, almost my home stage, and in front of the television cameras. Even now, 17 years later, most Brummies still know me as 'the driver who rolled in Sutton Park'.

The Saturday I retired saw Suzi Quatro climb to number one in the hit parade with *48 Crash*, and I'd been driving number 48. It seemed perversely appropriate to adopt 48 as my competition licence number, which I have to this day.

So 1973 came to a pretty disastrous end. Once again we had made the mistake of tackling too many events, doing the Mexico, *Motoring News* and Welsh Rally Championships. We won the latter early on in the year, although it was a matter of pride rather than any great publicity, but we neared the end of the season second in the *Motoring News* series but still to clinch the Mexico Championship. With two events to go I had a good chance of lifting the title, provided that I could take two victories. I won the Taunton Rally, the penultimate round of the series. But then the Arabs declared war on the Israelis, there was an oil crisis and a consequent petrol shortage, rallying came to a dead stop and the last event, the Virgo Galaxy, never happened. Nigel duly won the championship by one point and got his works drive for the following year. As it turned out, the result would have fallen in his favour anyway, because an RAC tribunal had ruled that the results of the Gwynedd Rally, which I had won earlier in the year, should be nullified, so I wouldn't have been able to catch Nigel even if that final rally had taken place.

On top of that, there was bad news on the sponsorship front: Brooklyn Garages had been immensely successful and were given the opportunity of becoming a Ford distributor. The small premises in Inkberrow were sold and the company moved to Redditch, lock, stock and barrel. Progress for them, but the move effectively tied up all the available capital and Brooklyn were unable to support my rallying. Not only had I lost the Mexico Championship, but I had lost my sponsor as well. Both Mike and Keith Hill have remained good friends ever since. They have both been very supportive and did manage to continue giving me token support the following year. I had free use of their workshop in Redditch to build a car, and they contributed £25 to every rally I contested, irrespective of whether I carried their name on the car or not. But the outlook for 1974 looked bleak.

2

The Andrews years

The main objective now was to find a sponsor. I did contest the Circuit of Ireland Rally in April of 1974 with Stuart Gray in the old Brooklyn Mexico, and finished third in class behind two RS2000s, but the petrol crisis meant that there was no other real rallying until June. Then I put together my first sponsorship proposal. I circulated 148 companies and PR agencies, outlining my intention to tackle the Castrol/*Autosport* and RAC Group 1 Rally Championships. I received replies from something like 40 or 50 companies, and I'll never forget the one from Philips Electrical: 'Thank you, we get many requests from charities of this type, however it is not our policy to support them,' it read. That was a real dampener.

One of the proposals landed on the desk of Derek Hill, a motoring journalist from the Midlands, who had already approached Andrews Industrial Equipment for support for a Formula 3 team and had been turned down. But 1974 was the company's tenth anniversary year and Andrews were keen to try something unusual to celebrate their decade in business. Already they were considering a proposal involving a hot-air balloon and, with a slogan like 'Heat for Hire', I think I would have been tempted to go for the balloon idea. Luckily for me, John Andrews didn't. Perhaps he had a crystal ball because that same balloon crashed at a show in Birmingham later in the year.

One of the major deciding factors was that several rounds of the Castrol/*Autosport* Championship started and finished in towns where Andrews had regional companies, and John saw it as a useful opportunity for putting together a programme which would link a number of the regional bases. There followed a heavy meeting at the office of Andrews, which was then located at the end of a row of Victorian terraced houses in Wolverhampton. It was a gruelling session, as John Andrews sat facing me, probing inquisitively, while the Managing Director Eric Johnson sat to one side and growled the occasional devastating question on the benefits of sponsorship, costs and so on.

After much wine had been consumed, we arrived at a one-year deal and John Andrews included something which I think all new and wary sponsors might consider, performance-related bonus payments. The sponsorship agreement was to pay me £1,000 up front to get the team going and have the car prepared. This was to be made up to £1,500 if I won any championship, and I was then paid on the basis of £20 for every event that I started, £20 for each class win and £20 for every finish. These were great incentives to produce good results. Even so, the year cost a good deal out of my own pocket. The car was acquired on hire purchase, because I couldn't afford to buy an RS2000 outright and, in fact, it wasn't paid for until three years later. So it was to be a year's rallying on credit, and effectively the start of the 'Andrews Era'.

First, though, there was a tantalizing interlude. One of the first events to take place after the fuel crisis in 1974 was the Welsh International rally. I was asked by Tony Fall, then competitions manager for the Dealer Opel Team, if I would contest it in a Group 1 Ascona 1.9S, with Richard Hudson-Evans in the co-driver's seat. DOT had just been set up and Fall was looking for a driver. This was an opportunity for me to become involved with a factory team, and Tony dangled a carrot by saying that at the end of the year there would be an opportunity to drive one of the 16-valve Ascona Group A rally cars which Walter Röhrl had just started to campaign in Germany. (It has to be said, these didn't have a very impressive reputation at the time.)

I tackled the Welsh, finishing third in Group 1, and with the points I had already scored on the Mintex and Circuit of Ireland rallies, held a sizable lead in the Group 1 category of the championship. Richard Hudson-Evans had brought a film crew along with him to cover Opel's

This RS2000, registration number BUY 22M, was the first car to carry the Andrews Heat for Hire livery and brought Russell some of his most notable early successes. Here it is being pushed hard through the lanes of County Donegal on the 1974 Tour of Donegal Rally.

involvement in rallying, and at the end of the Welsh, Tony Fall decided to apply the pressure: I was asked to meet him on the seafront at Barry where the rally finished and, in front of the cameras, was offered a works drive in an Opel Ascona. It put me in a very difficult position. My analysis was that, although the car wouldn't be capable of winning the Group 1 category on any of the remaining events, the points I'd already scored would enable me to win the RAC Group 1 championship. But I could foresee a situation arising at the end of the year where I would be offered the Group A car, but then the Group 1 championship would be deemed too important and the offer would never actually come to fruition.

I was forced to make a very quick decision and with some regret I declined Tony's offer. I imagine that was one bit of film that was not used on television! The drive, in fact, went to Tony Pond and he made great use of it, but the Group 1 project was dropped and he went on to achieve greater publicity in the Group A Ascona.

Because of the petrol crisis my season with Andrews

didn't really start until half-way through the year, and the first event that I contested was the 1974 Tour of Donegal Rally, with John Brown alongside. This was part of the Castrol/*Autosport* Championship. After a rally-long battle with Robin Eyre-Maunsell in his Group 1 Avenger, Robin tipped the car on to its side on some moorland, and I ran out the winner of Group 1 in eighth place overall. We then went on to contest a whole series of events that year, of which the highlight was the Castrol 75 Rally (Castrol's 75th anniversary was celebrated in 1974). Against tough opposition, I managed to finish second overall in a Group 1 car, which attracted a lot of publicity. The winner was Tony Drummond in a BDA Escort, but we had won the Group 1 Championship.

I then wanted to contest the RAC Rally, but the car that I had been using had gone through a very hard time. Leaving the successes aside, there had also been a fair number of crashes as well. It was in a pretty sorry state approaching the RAC Rally, and I explained the predicament to Stuart Turner at Ford. Between us, we

he would be prepared to support me in a works BDA-powered rally car for the coming season. Ford had agreed to loan me a car and most of the parts if I could find the running costs.

I had also been offered the Kleber Scholarship. Drivers had the opportunity of using a works car with Kleber support on selected European events. Past winners had been Chris Sclater in 1974 and Billy Coleman in 1973. The opportunity was downgraded a little in '75, in that instead of a Ford Escort BDA the car to be used was a Datsun 160J. I also had an offer from British Leyland for a four or five-rally programme in a works Dolomite Sprint. They had eventually woken up to the fact that an employee (they owned Land Rover then) had shown talent in rallying circles. In addition, Des O'Dell asked me to drive a Group 1 Avenger and Vauxhall offered a paid drive in a Magnum. I therefore had the opportunity, very unusual for a young driver, of five possible works cars.

I considered them all in depth: the Datsun didn't seem an attractive proposition as I felt that it wouldn't be

The Escort RS2000 on the Castrol 75 Rally, which celebrated the lubricant company's 75th anniversary in 1974.

worked out a solution unique in Ford's history. Stuart agreed to let me buy a car on a one year, credit free sale. The problem was that by the time the decision had been passed, there was insufficient time left to build a rally car in the usual way. We then hit upon a scheme, with the co-operation of Ford Advanced Vehicle Operations, whereby we would take all the competition components down to the Aveley plant, and on Friday evening Bill Meade and Charlie Mead stood on the side of the production line and gave the workers the appropriate bits to use in place of the standard components. So GVX 833N was created in unprecedented circumstances. It came off the production line as a runner already in basic rally spec, and was taken home that night, shortening the build time by up to two weeks. It would have been great to say that the end result was something special, but the gearbox eventually broke on the RAC Rally, in a Penmachno stage.

At the end of 1974, Andrews were very pleased with the outcome of the rallying that year and the publicity that they had achieved. In turn, I asked John Andrews if

reliable because of underdevelopment, the Dolomite Sprint deal came with a very limited programme and, since I really wanted to get out of Group 1, the Magnum and Avenger drives didn't appeal either. I have always felt that you should go for the competitive drive rather than the money, because in the long run that is the best thing to achieve. Without results your long term future isn't there. So it was then that I accepted the offer from Stuart Turner of a loaned car. Although more difficult financially, this proved to be the correct decision in the long term.

A deal was put together with the *Birmingham Post* and the car ran in a joint colour scheme. It was because of this association between Andrews and the *Post* that the Andrews Heat for Hire yellow livery came into being. ICI 'Truck Yellow' was actually the colour of *Birmingham Post* delivery vans. I have never been at such difficult negotiations in all my life. The Editor of the *Birmingham Post*, Maurice Bright, and John Andrews had to resolve how the car should be painted: should it be the red, silver and blue of Andrews or the yellow and white of the *Birmingham Post*? Should the colours be split lengthways

Notable cars of the Andrews Years. The BDA-powered Escort RS1800 was Russell's first top-flight rally machine. STW 129R is here on its way to second place on the 1978 Mintex International Rally.

Des O'Dell, Talbot Competitions Director, and Russell pose beside the works-assisted Talbot Sunbeam Lotus outside the Ryton plant. The Talbot was the first pretender to the Escort's rallying crown.

Fast and reliable, the Vauxhall Chevette HSR helped Russell to many successes in the early 1980s. Victories came on tarmac in the West Cork and Circuit of Ireland rallies, but the car was also good in the forests, as here.

The Opel Manta brought Russell some of his finest results, although in the forests it struggled to match the new generation of four-wheel-drive machinery.

The Vauxhall Astra (or Opel Kadett), seen below right on the Manx Rally, wasn't particularly competitive, but Russell used one to come within one second of winning the 1987 Marlboro National Rally Championship.

The Lancia Delta (above) on the 1987 Lombard RAC Rally gave Russell his first taste of four-wheel-drive rallying and one of his best chances of winning the event.

Russell drove superbly in 1989 in the Mike Little Ford Sierra RS Cosworth and finished second to David Llewellin in the Shell British Open Rally Championship.

31

or top to bottom? Eventually the whole matter was resolved on the toss of a coin, that Andrews should have the blue only and the *Post* should have the yellow. A coin was tossed again to determine which company's colour went on top.

There was now enough money to employ one full-time mechanic and an advert recruited Ricky Bell. A cockney at heart, he had plenty of experience with works teams around Europe. Fortunately he was happy to work on his own, as he was stuck in a rented corner of Goodbrook Motors for long periods, often late into the night, for most of the year. Allen Goodall certainly complained about the increase in his phone bill at the time! Ricky was then joined by Paul Ridgway. I don't think it could have been possible to have two more enthusiastic workers than those two that year.

With the RS2000 decked out in the new colour scheme, John Brown and myself tackled the Circuit of Ireland Rally. We finished fifth overall and first in Group 1, despite blowing the head gasket on the third stage, which meant that it was necessary to top up the engine with water at the start and finish of each stage. I'll never forget one of John's skills coming to the fore on that event. For all his rallymanship, he was an extremely honest competitor and certainly never resorted to cheating in any form: I soon learned to appreciate the difference between rallymanship and cheating during that Circuit of Ireland.

We had a rally-long battle with Harold Morley in a Porsche, co-driven by Rupert Saunders. It became clear that as we commenced the run back up from Killarney, Harold would pass us and take fifth place. There was one

long, 32-mile stage still to attempt across Sally Gap and so we spread the story around that we were actually going to have a pitstop during the stage to replenish the water that was still gushing out of the engine. John persuaded the marshal at the start of the stage to let us start the test two minutes behind Harold. He had been sitting near the finish line of each stage in an attempt to collect our stage times and automatically assumed that we had recorded a time 48 seconds slower than himself, and not 12 seconds quicker as it was in reality. The ruse was completed at the breakfast halt when John Brown was asked by Rupert Saunders what our time had been on the stage and he refused to give it.

Results services in those days were not as they are today and it was impossible to find out any information other than through fellow competitors. John then wrote down a series of times from the last few stages on the back of his road book, including the fictitious time. When we went off to breakfast and locked the car, John left the book on top of the dashboard with the times showing. As we sat down to eat we saw Rupert Saunders nosing around the car and peering through the window at the times on the back of the roadbook. He obviously thought that John had made a mistake by leaving them visible. Of course he then took them as gospel. We continued very hard for the remainder of the rally, with Harold confident in the knowledge that he had built up a 48-second gap over us. On the last few stages, while he drove very steadily, we speeded up and snatched fifth place by fifteen seconds. Needless to say they were both very upset at the time, but it satisfied John's sense of honesty because in fact he had not told a lie.

Escort on tarmac: Russell and John Brown forge on through typical Irish terrain.

Russell pushes the Andrews Escort to the limit on the way to an impressive victory on the 1976 Scottish rally.

On my next event, the Granite City Rally, I drove an old works RS1600 (with the famous registration number OOO 96M) as the new Mk2 was not ready. The first event in the new car was the Welsh International, which was the rally where John made a rather serious mistake by booking me into a time control early. What could so easily have been a win turned out to be just fifth overall.

A number of other events that season failed to realize the promise I had shown earlier in the season, including an almost disastrous Avon Tour of Britain, won that year by Roger Clark. Julia, my wife, thought that Ricky Bell was a bit lonely and, as a bit of matchmaking, introduced him to Sue, a beautiful blonde. For about a month – the period of time when the Avon Tour car should have been prepared – Ricky just couldn't concentrate on the matter in hand, and he nearly missed every service point on the event, despite the relaxed schedule. He was stopping at each phone box en route to call Sue!

After a very shaky start on the RAC Rally we found ourselves challenging Roger Clark for second place. One

Opposite: Russell trying hard on the Great Orme special stage near Llandudno in North Wales.

In the dead of night, the Andrews Escort at a service point.

of the problems Ford had in those days was the inferior material used in the manufacture of the wheel studs. It was necessary to get out of the car before the start of every stage and torque them up very accurately. In the rush to get through Kielder we omitted to do this on one occasion and the wheel studs broke half-way through a stage. It was a great disappointment, as we found out later that we had just passed Roger Clark and were challenging Timo Mäkinen for first overall. Sadly, it all came to nothing.

John Andrews and his wife Jill have always taken a deep interest in my career and there was a very peculiar occurrence on this RAC Rally. It had been very exciting for everyone in Andrews at the time, but Jill Andrews had a premonition that we would not in fact finish the event. This was not related to me until some time after the rally, but apparently at a few minutes past three in the morning Jill woke and told her husband that we had retired from the rally. At first he didn't believe her. It wasn't until about two months later, when the Boreham mechanics were cleaning out my rally car, that they came across various bits and pieces which were put into an envelope

and sent to me. These included the time card for the stage on which we retired. According to the card we started the test at precisely three in the morning and retired somewhere half-way through a ten minute stage. Hence we retired at five minutes past three. It seems amazing but John had made a note in his diary that Jill had woken him up at 3.06 to tell him that we were out.

The *Birmingham Post* decided not to continue in 1976 and, by December, John Andrews hadn't come to grips with the sums of money required to run a works-spec car for a full season, the budget for 1976 being £8,000. I then decided to organize a rally forum at Bristol Street Motors, with whom I was also in discussion at the time. Stuart Turner was in the chair, along with guests Roger Clark, Jackie Stewart and Ken Tyrrell (who'd brought his six-wheeled Formula 1 car). The *Birmingham Post* guaranteed publicity and on the night there were between five and six thousand people crowding the showrooms and spilling out on to the street. It was exciting chaos, as we held a forum in the conference rooms and a second off the stairs in the main showroom, with loudspeakers relaying the chat to those outside.

Bristol Street Motors were impressed, but I think John Andrews' competitive spirit took hold and he soon agreed to fund the 1976 programme, rather than let any car salesmen take over 'his deal'. Although we no longer had support from the *Birmingham Post*, we looked through all the photographs from that year and came to the conclusion that the yellow of the rally car stood out well, so Andrews adopted the colour for my rally programme.

At the Ford Motorsport press conference at the start of 1976, Stuart Turner was under pressure from numerous British journalists, asking him why the company hadn't taken on any young British drivers and if there was any chance that they would do so. He stated that in his opinion no young British driver around was capable of beating a works driver and, consequently, none of them deserved a place in the factory team. Martin Holmes got up, dangled the bait and suggested that Stuart wouldn't mind offering a works drive on those terms because he had a safe bet.

The Talbot Sunbeam Lotus runs wide at a hairpin. Mechanical unreliability dogged Russell's efforts with this car, but he did manage fourth on the 1980 RAC Rally and third on the Welsh.

Cutaway reveals the details of the Andrews Talbot Sunbeam used in 1980 and 1981. The 16-valve twin-cam Lotus engine drove the rear wheels through a live axle in an overall layout not radically different from that of the all-conquering RS Escort.

It could only be in Ireland: under the placid gaze of local spectators, the Sunbeam lifts an inside front wheel on the Circuit of Ireland Rally.

So Stuart Turner then made his famous promise that if a young driver came along and beat a works driver in a straight fight on an international rally, and won the event, he would be given a works drive for the following year. That statement was quoted in many of the motoring publications. On the 1976 Scottish Rally, in a struggle with Ari Vatanen and Roger Clark, I had the satisfaction of holding Stuart Turner to his promise. At the end of 1976 I was duly offered a works Ford drive for the coming season, which I accepted with great pleasure. So ended a year which saw my first national and international rally wins, on the Granite City and Scottish rallies respectively.

In 1977 I handed in my notice at Land Rover. They found it difficult to find a replacement for my post and asked if I would stay on for three months, accepting the fact that I might ask for quite a few days off, but requesting that I did not abuse the position. I was in the unique situation where I was a works Ford driver and also an employee of British Leyland! It worked out incredibly

well because my last pay packet came at a time when BL was in great turmoil. I had a pay rise backdated for 18 months, which I would not have been given had I left straight away.

Looking at the rallying scene nowadays, it is difficult to appreciate how competitive the sport was in the late 1970s. My major opposition in 1977 and '78 came from Roger Clark, Björn Waldegaard, John Taylor and Ari Vatanen in similar works Ford cars, Hannu Mikkola in a factory Toyota, Markku Alen in a Fiat, Pentti Airikkala in a Chevette and Tony Pond in the works TR7. There is no longer that level of factory support in the British championship.

The main feature of the year was my battle with Airikkala. The narrow winning margins on some of the rallies were quite amazing: I won two rallies by a mere second, I beat him on the Ulster Rally by six seconds and he beat me on the Castrol Rally by a little over twenty. The championship in those days used to conclude with

37

the RAC International Rally. I finished third overall after a fairly fraught drive and that was enough to clinch the first Open Rally Championship.

In some ways 1976 and 1977 were highlights of my association with Andrews. A friend and former Rover engineer, Peter Harrison, had been persuaded to join the team after Ricky Bell moved to Talbot, and we set up a workshop inside the Andrews factory where, after taking over the first Mk2 Escort, Peter built a tarmac specification car (which won the 1976 Scottish Rally). Special components were made by the Engineering Department within Andrews and the situation produced a really close relationship between the staff and the rally team, encouraged by the enthusiastic support of the Advertising and Marketing Manager, David Cooper. It was also a period of major growth for the company which was lucky for me.

In contrast, the following year brought great disappointment. For several seasons I had followed a steady path of progress with Ford, but I feel that my significant results failed to gain the recognition that they deserved. Perhaps the year started on the wrong footing, as Stuart Turner asked me to attend a meeting early on and told me that he wanted me to take a different co-driver, one whom I think Ford would have found more malleable. After a quiet, but tense, discussion I won the day, as I feel that the driver should always be able to choose his co-driver. Besides, I can be very stubborn, but a 'head-to-head' was probably not the most political way of handling the situation.

Again I contested the British Open Championship and a number of other events, including the New Zealand Rally and a couple of rallies in Europe. I didn't win the series again: after a season-long battle with Hannu Mikkola the championship was resolved on the Burmah International Rally. Coming into the last stage we had

something in the order of a minute and three-quarters lead over Hannu, which was good going on a short event. Then catastrophe struck on the Ardgarten stage when the engine crossmember broke and the powerplant dropped on to the steering column. The result was that you could only steer left or right, not straight ahead. We negotiated the remainder of the stage in a series of slow swerves, arrived at the end of the test and discovered that Hannu had taken precisely one minute and forty-five seconds from us. So we finished the rally on equal times, but the tie-decider went in favour of whoever was quickest on the last stage. The finish marshal withstood a prolonged, and almost persuasive, barrage from my co-driver Peter Bryant, determined to gain one second.

It was then that I had a most unusual proposition. Hannu, now effectively the British Champion, had dashed off before the prizegiving to contest another rally and this upset the organizers a great deal. At one time there was an offer on the table to cancel the appropriate stage and allow me to win the event. Happily this did not come to fruition.

I also won the Circuit of Ireland Rally that year after a very exciting drive. We had one of Ford's new, tarmac specification, fuel-injection cars. John Brown was trying to read the road off the maps on the Knocka hillclimb, but called a hairpin right 'absolutely flat' by mistake. We bowled into this hairpin at about 80mph, demolished the drystone wall opposite and landed in a field. By chance the car was still a runner, albeit extremely battered and losing water, but the big problem was that there was no gate out of the field. We were forced to demolish the wall to extricate ourselves and hare down the stage to the finish for service. At this point I felt that Ford lost a little interest, for it took the mechanics quite a few service points to restore the car to anything like a suitable condition. But perhaps that was a reflection of the level of damage!

Russell considers the Vauxhall Chevette to be one of the finest-handling rally cars he has driven. Above, a sponsors' photo-call and right, a service point on the 1982 Manx Rally.

Hannu Mikkola had already retired as we set off into the west of Ireland on a vile, rainy night. We made what turned out to be a shrewd decision, fitting A2 forest tyres to the car for the tarmac stages which were streaming with water. As we arrived at Killarney we found ourselves back in second place, having pulled in the region of eight or nine minutes off the rest of the competitors during the one night. This was a lesson which I have benefited from on several occasions since. I always insist that tyre crews take at least one set of wide forest tyres for use in just those conditions. If the roads are awash it doesn't matter

how many cuts you have in racing tyres, they will not cope with deep water.

It was also a difficult year because it marked the end of my time with John Brown. He had come under a lot of pressure at work and was not putting the level of attention which was required into his rallying. Consequently, he made a number of rather silly mistakes which, as with many co-driver errors, can be catastrophic. On a number of occasions I was booked into time controls either early or late. It was just a simple matter of inattention or bad calculation. Thankfully, our personal friendship still

Sixth overall on the 1,000 Lakes Rally in 1982 was the best result ever achieved on the Finnish event by a non-Scandinavian at the time.

The Chevette proved successful for Russell on the Circuit of Ireland: he followed up a second place in 1982 with victory the following year.

Rallysprints were common events in the early 1980s. This is Russell's Chevette on the 1982 Rothmans National Rallysprint at Longleat.

Russell balancing the slide with the Chevette on full song during the 1983 Scottish Rally.

remains, but we decided to part in rallying after the Scottish Rally that year.

I won the New Zealand Rally with Ford, and also the Dutch Tulip Rally with Peter Bryant. I finished the year having won three international events, an equal first on the Burmah and second in the British Championship. I thought that things looked interesting for 1979. The offer on the table from Ford was up to four works outings in the World Championship, including the Monte Carlo and Acropolis rallies. This was eventually downgraded to doing those events in a Ford Fiesta, as part of the development programme for the new car, and the ultimate outcome was that I did the British series again in a works car for the tarmac rallies and a loaned car for the forest events, looked after by our own mechanic, Peter Harrison. As has so often been the case with Ford, what started out to be of great promise dropped by the wayside. I often wonder if British drivers are given a fair crack of the whip, because when foreign drivers work for Ford they are not in a position to put together their own service teams, so Ford are forced to undertake everything. I wonder if they appreciate how demoralizing it is when what starts out as a 'full works drive' for a Briton becomes a 'works assisted drive' with many of the pressures and organizational problems having to be borne by the driver himself.

Undoubtedly the highspots of 1979 were winning the Manx International Rally and finishing second on the RAC Rally. I may have ended the latter event some way behind Hannu Mikkola, but I took great pride in seeing the likes of Timo Salonen, Björn Waldegaard and Ari Vatanen behind me! It was also the end of the first Boreham era, in that the factory decided to pull the plug on its mainstream rallying programme following the demise of the Mk2 Escort. They have yet to return to the top flight even now, although we wait to see what happens with the Sierra Cosworth 4x4.

I had agreed to join Talbot shortly after the Manx Rally in 1979 and had discussed with their competition boss, Des O'Dell, a planned season that included the British Championship, RAC, Sanremo, Ypres and Acropolis rallies and some other events in Europe. Des made a great show of sacking Tony Pond on television after his retirement on the RAC, but must have made his mind up well before that in the light of the programme that I was offered. I think it was inevitable that two such characters should eventually fall out. Sadly, my programme was reduced dramatically when Peugeot took over Talbot early that year, but at least the salary was agreed, and was not surpassed for many seasons. That was some consolation for my disappointment.

The Talbot Sunbeam Lotus was still a relatively new proposition. I had a number of good drives early in the year, including leading the Mintex before the crank seized, and a win on the Sunday Run of the Circuit of Ireland after we had taken the engine out of Henri

After the Chevette came another GM car, the Opel Manta. The 1984 Manx Rally was not one of Russell's most memorable occasions, but here he overtakes Per Eklund's Toyota at the Sartfield Hairpin.

Russell, partnered by Mike Broad, pushes the Manta to the limit through the tight lanes of the Isle of Man.

Toivonen's crashed car to replace our blown unit. Retirements marred the rest of the British series, although I finished fourth on the RAC Rally after a battle with Henri Toivonen, Hannu Mikkola and Guy Fréquelin. My performance was hampered by a series of punctures and broken shock absorbers.

The Talbot association was outstandingly good from the Andrews point of view, because the sponsorship really seemed to open doors at the Talbot factories. I always found it surprising that General Motors and Ford never expanded the association between its rally teams and the other factory departments, even just to the extent of helping sponsors to talk to the right people or at least produce some recognition. Andrews always moved its fleet car buying policy in line with the rally team and, at

Talbot, reciprocally, sales of Andrews' equipment into the factories increased dramatically.

Looking round at the start of 1981, I realized that rallying was going to change significantly. The regulations had been altered to allow the use of four-wheel drive cars and Audi were the first on the scene with their revolutionary Quattro. At first no one thought that it could be competitive but they were silenced when the team convincingly won the Swedish Rally with Hannu Mikkola. I had already been talking to Audi, through the British importer, with a view to using the car in the Open Rally Championship. We felt the need to do something different and I was convinced, after talks with Hannu, that this would be a very successful car. As it turned out, though, the Audi team had a fairly disastrous run for the rest of the year.

Note the number of spectators as Russell pushes on over the tarmac roads of the Epynt ranges on the 1984 Welsh Rally.

The Opel kicks up the dust on a forest stage on the Welsh International.

Brookes charges through a watersplash en route to a top-10 finish in the Opel Manta on the 1984 RAC Rally.

Victory on the 1985 Manx International was sufficient to clinch Russell's second British Open Championship.

Flying through Scotland: the Manta was used to good effect on the Scottish Rally in 1984, 1985 and 1986.

The Scottish Rally, opposite, has a reputation for offering rocky terrain. Here, the Manta copes admirably with typical surfaces.

This shot of the Opel Manta in the snow, right, provided Andrews with an ideal Christmas card in 1985. In contrast, the temperature in the cockpit reached 150 degrees F during the Cyprus Rally, below.

I began negotiations with Audi's competition manager, Walter Treser, reaching the point where I was offered the use of an Audi in this country. Amazingly, after I had journeyed to Ingolstadt to see my car being built, and after I had spent time testing with the team at Vallelunga, the whole agreement was dramatically and inexplicably cancelled in March. I was bitterly disappointed, because this would have been the perfect opportunity to try something new.

I have never truly discovered the reason why the deal was quashed. It may have been that Audi were finding it difficult to support an extra car and the drain on the resources was too great. On the other hand, Rothmans had become involved. They were already sponsoring the British Championship, a Ford team with Malcolm Wilson and Pentti Airikkala, and a World programme with Ari Vatanen. In February, Pentti had won the Mintex International for them, strengthening their chances of victory in the British Championship, but Hannu had dominated the Swedish Rally in the new Audi. Rothmans, obviously worried about the competitiveness of the new car, approached Audi with a view to obtaining a Quattro for the 1982 season. It was after this deal had been discussed that I lost my chance to drive a Quattro in 1981!

So at the very last moment I found myself without a drive. Des O'Dell came to my rescue and made a car available, with preparation to be undertaken by Mike Little. I also teamed up with a new co-driver, Mike Broad.

Despite some success, the two years driving a Talbot were very frustrating. In 1980 I had contested 10 events, but of those rallies I only finished three, retiring six times with mechanical failures. 1981 only produced two finishes in international rallies. In many ways this was a low point in my rallying career and, apart from odd flashes, I think that my driving reflected all the setbacks and generally lacked sparkle.

In 1982 the opportunity arose to join the newly-formed GM Dealer Sport team. Dealer Opel Team (DOT) and Dealer Team Vauxhall (DTV) had previously worked as separate units but, with the amalgamation of the dealer network, it was decided to set up one organization. The team was going to continue to run the Chevette, after a major season the previous year with Tony Pond.

This was a really busy time. In December 1982, Julia and I moved from Inkberrow to Besford, a hamlet near Pershore in Worcestershire. Around the same time a long-standing schoolfriend, Andrew Smith, said to me 'How many people have asked you when you are going to open a garage or something similar? All the people you know in motorsport are in advertising, promotions and the like: they all place print orders. I think you should start a printing company!' From the initial idea in November, through the acquisition of premises, people and machinery, to producing the first jobs in late February seemed a very hectic period, but we got it all done and set up a company of which I am very proud. Amongst those first contracts were GM Dealer Sport News, and work for the Thor Hammer Company (one time sponsors of Will Sparrow's Mini).

I duly joined the Blydenstein GM organization alongside Terry Kaby. In some ways the next two years, although not particularly successful in terms of results, were just what I needed after the 1981 season of unreliability. By 1983 I had contested 25 events in the Chevette, including rallysprints. The fact that I only retired on one through mechanical problems was a great boost to my confidence. I also tackled a number of overseas events that year with Ronan Morgan, including taking victory on the West Cork Rally, second in Haspengouw, third on the Hunsrück Rally and sixth on the 1,000 Lakes, the latter tackled on a shoestring budget.

At that time sixth was the highest a non-Scandinavian

Desert scene, opposite: the Raid Paris–Dakar, on which Russell drove a MAN truck for Opel in 1986, provided a new and unforgettable environment.

Russell's last win in the Manta came on the 1987 Welsh Rally. This was the last international victory for the car – and its first on an international forest rally!

had ever finished on the Finnish event. The car was by now underpowered and we only had one service van and chase vehicle at our disposal. I cut down costs by doing the recce in a borrowed Vauxhall Cavalier; we towed a caravan behind it through the stages and slept by the roadside at night.

In 1983 I tackled the British series again in a Chevette, before moving over to the Opel Manta the following year. Thus began the big rivalry with Jimmy McRae. 1984 was something of a learning year for me, and I finished second in the championship behind Jimmy, but this paved the way for a classic confrontation in 1985.

I don't think the fans of rallying were disappointed, though the year also had some fairly traumatic moments in it for me. On the Circuit of Ireland Rally, General Motors took an inexplicable decision, half-way through the Sunday run when I was leading the event by a handful of seconds from Jimmy McRae, to issue team orders. Jimmy was allowed to win the event and I finished second, ostensibly with a view to improving Jimmy's chances of finishing in the top five of the European Championship. As the Circuit was only a coefficient one or two event I couldn't see the reasoning behind the decision.

It certainly caused a few difficulties with sponsors. Although General Motors promised to return the favour later in the year, John Andrews quite rightly pointed out that he was in the business to win and that we had been deprived of a victory and the publicity attached to it. At the restart on the Monday we decided to get the deed over and done with, and duly sat on the start line of the first stage for thirty seconds after the flag had dropped. We marked time behind Jimmy, but the situation got to me and at the end of the section we had a very hard push through the Mourne mountains on the way back to Belfast. I arrived at the rest halt one second in the lead. I was then firmly pointed in the direction of a pile of forest tyres and told that if I didn't slow down the car would be fitted up with them.

As it turned out, there was never any need to return the favour. Despite a year-long battle with Jimmy, we gradually gained the upper hand. This came to a head on the Ulster Rally where we won by sixteen seconds, leaving just the Manx International between me and a second Open Championship. Early on in the rally I collected a puncture, which was fairly catastrophic in that it cost me nearly three minutes. General Motors were in a quandary when, on the final day, Jimmy was leading the rally. The gap was still substantial and they couldn't bring themselves to hold him back. It was even doubtful whether Jimmy would have agreed to their team orders, and I couldn't have blamed him in the slightest. With three stages to go the lead was whittled down to one second, then the situation was resolved when a shock absorber mounting broke on Jimmy's car and chopped the fuel pump wires in half. He was brought to a time-consuming stop for nearly ten minutes. I think there was a great sigh of relief breathed among the General Motors management.

The following year, 1986, started out with much promise but came to nothing. I appreciated that the Astra was not going to be competitive, but there had been the promise of the Astra 4S, the four-wheel-drive machine that Opel were developing, and I decided to have a year marking time in the hope that the new car would be highly competitive. It was also the year of Henri Toivonen's fatal crash in Corsica, and the dramatic changes in the regulations for rallying resulting from the growing worries about safety. In the middle of the season, FISA's decision to cancel Group B and Group S meant that the whole of GM's Group S project with the Astra was knocked on the head and the car never came to fruition.

Indirectly this decision gave me what is probably my most memorable rally. At the start of 1986 I had contested the British Truck Grand Prix for Renault in an R280 and finished second in the small-capacity final. Tony Fall, GM Europe's competition boss, was looking

The only official British outing for the four-wheel-drive Astra 4S was in the hands of Andrew Wood on the 1986 Audi Sport Rally, and it arguably cost him the National Championship.

for a fast driver to pilot a chase truck on the Paris–Dakar Raid and assumed that because I had driven in the Truck Grand Prix I must have had an HGV licence.

Although the offer came during the RAC Rally, with just four weeks to go before the truck needed to be collected, I didn't disillusion Tony, and set about obtaining my licence. I passed the test on December 23 and flew out to Germany on Boxing Day to collect the 350bhp MAN 6x6 (with seven tons of spares on board) to take part in one of the greatest adventures ever devised and, as it turned out, the last of the old style Paris–Dakar Raids.

FISA's decision to outlaw Group B and Group S made it very difficult for me to obtain a competitive drive for the following year. I did the majority of the British National series in a Vauxhall Astra, and all but clinched

the Group A category on the Audi Sport Rally, had it not been for Trevor Smith winning through by a mere second. It was also a year of marking time in the Opel Manta, when it became clear that the Sierra Cosworth was now a force to be reckoned with, Jimmy McRae winning the Circuit of Ireland for the fourth time on his first outing in the R-E-D-prepared Sierra.

I managed to win the Welsh Rally in the Manta. As so often happens in the sport, the car gets to the end of its competitive life just as it reaches the ultimate peak of development. That was the best forest Manta we had ever used and the Welsh win seemed to come so easily because I was so utterly relaxed with the car. If only one could shorten the development time of such cars there would be so many benefits to be gained.

After changing international regulations outlawed the 4S project, GM could only rally the front-wheel-drive Astra GTE. This is Russell on the 1987 Scottish Rally.

The Vauxhall Astra was never going to be a serious match for more powerful cars, but on the 1987 Rothmans Circuit of Ireland Rally, Russell held second place for a time.

The 1987 Circuit of Ireland again: Russell takes the tightest possible line.

Driven with considerable verve, the Vauxhall Astra took Russell very close indeed to the National Championship title in 1987.

It was clear that I had to do something to add some sparkle to my rally programme and develop some interest for the sponsors, so I decided to put something together for the RAC Rally. The last thing I wanted was to tackle the RAC in a Vauxhall Astra. The Lancia Delta Integrale was the most competitive car around, and I discussed with several people how I could best go about getting hold of a works Lancia for the RAC. There were conflicting views: some said that you needed the support of Lancia UK and should go through them, and others said that you needed to try through David Richards because he organized the service for them on that event and knew them well. I happened to meet Neil Wilson again: he had co-driven for me once before, back in the days of the Mexico Championship. I rang Neil and he came out, in the way that only Neil can, with the simple solution that I should ring Cesare Fiorio, Lancia's competition boss. Neil said that the man spoke very good English, he was sure that he would know of me and my performances on the RAC

Rally, and that there was nothing to be lost by trying. At worst he could only say no.

So, in May of 1987, I rang Fiorio and he expressed some interest in the idea, although he wanted until July to think about it. I then flew over to see him in July, and in a meeting which took all of four minutes he agreed to supply a works Lancia. I made it an absolute requirement of the deal that it should be a works car and not a Jolly Club one, which he was agreeable to. The whole plan took shape very smoothly and very rapidly, and we had a fully competitive works car. It was a great opportunity to do well on the RAC, and from the sponsor's point of view it provided outstanding television and media interest. I was the only British driver to use a car from Abarth, the Fiat/Lancia competition department, since 1976 when Vic Elford drove one.

Joining the team as a very enthusiastic member of the service crew was Andrew Fitton. We had first met in 1980, when Andrew was a motorsport co-ordinator for

Driving Force was a pro-celebrity competition put on for the benefit of television in 1987. It saw Russell teamed with actor Nigel Havers to handle a variety of unlikely vehicles including a fire engine. . .

and a tank, here with former racing driver Stirling Moss gathering the reactions of the crew.

Full line-up for *Driving Force*, flanking the army instructor, was, from the left, Lennie Bennett, Martin Brundle, Nigel Havers, Russell Brookes, Mike Smith, Barrie Sheene, Roger Daltry, Gina Campbell and Lesley Ash.

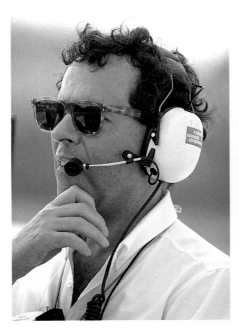

The car to have in 1987 was a Lancia Delta, and if you wanted one of those you went to Cesare Fiorio, above left, then overseeing the Lancia Abarth rally programme. The one-off outing on the 1987 RAC Rally gave Russell his most competitive mount for some time. Scenes from the rally include an evocative night shot, opposite, and the watersplash in Trentham Gardens.

Castrol. Since those times he had built up a reputation for putting together successful deals in the City and, in 1986, had set out to build the name of Braithwaite Engineering. The first major acquisition was the Andrews Group in May 1987. The stock market crash of October 1987 made the City a pretty unexciting place for a time, so Andrew became more closely involved in the running of the company, and enthusiastically joined in the motorsport programme.

The event was not a success, however, for I had grossly underestimated the problems of swapping to a left-hand-drive car. Although you can achieve 95% of the performance very easily, the last five per cent is very difficult to extract. You are so conditioned to driving a right-hand-drive car that you don't naturally position the left-hooker correctly. I found that when my concentration lapsed just a little, I subconsciously tried to place the car a few inches more and more to the right-hand side of the road to equate to the view of the road as I would normally see it from the right-hand seat.

We were caught out in Kielder forest after taking a couple of fastest times. We came to a stage which was very slippery and particularly narrow with just two tram lines through the gravel. I was running with the wheels on the verges and not in the tram lines. As I touched the brakes on one corner the car skated off the road and into a ditch: the damage was beyond repair. But the whole package had been great experience and I came away very impressed with the way the Italian team was organized both in terms of enthusiasm and in their attention to detail preparation.

The Italian service crews work differently from our mechanics. In Turin there is a department devoted to

assembling the tools for the mechanics, and on the Sanremo Rally, for example, one van delivered all the tool chests at the start and each mechanic signed for his equipment. This department puts together the spanners required for the particular car build: if something has changed on a car since the previous rally, the tool content is changed to suit, and if specific small spares are needed they are put into the boxes as well. It was details like those which made the organization so impressive.

John Andrews was unsure about the publicity benefits to be gained from doing another British Championship in a mediocre car in 1988. As far as Andrews were concerned, the RAC Rally had attracted massive publicity, probably the most for ten years. Understandably it was a hard act to follow and he decided to sit aside from the sport for a period to see what would develop.

During that year I came together with Mike Little again (Mike had prepared the Talbot in 1981) to run a Sierra RS Cosworth and when it came to the RAC Rally, John Andrews decided that, in view of the engine's record of unreliability, I should carefully run it in myself, as a matter of policy. Doing just that, during a sedate tour of West Cumbria, I noticed how many old factories there were, no doubt all without modern heating systems, and without an Andrews depot in reach! After putting the idea to John Andrews, Mike Little took over an Andrews franchise...

Mike Little then put together a package of five rallies in the Sierra Cosworth and Neil Wilson joined me as co-driver. As well as providing a chance to try the new-generation Ford, this short, six-month programme also gave me the oportunity of looking at alternative suppliers.

Until then people had mostly been running Pirelli or Michelin tyres, but I decided to approach Dunlop. I have always had a very high regard for their products and it seemed that they were making a substantial comeback in the racing world. Their tyres for the forests were seemingly dated in design, but turned out to be far more competitive than anyone else realized. It is quite surprising that the forest tyres we are successfully using now were first introduced in 1979.

I quickly adapted to the Sierra and finished third on the Scottish Rally, despite a time-consuming off and the disadvantage of having only a soft-compound tyre, which was the only one available in this country at the time. Our testing and development all came to fruition when we won the Audi Sport Rally, having at one stage led Timo Salonen and Hannu Mikkola in the factory Mazdas and beaten Stig Blomqvist in the works Sierra.

or whether it was now time to think of other things. I came back from the sabbatical knowing that I still really wanted to drive rally cars, and with renewed enthusiasm, which was reflected in my driving. Also I had a co-driver, in Neil Wilson, who really appreciated the psychology of how to make a driver go quicker. He recognized that on many occasions the last thing that a driver needs is to be wound up, it is more important to relax him and break down tensions which inhibit good, flowing performances.

I talked to Andrew Fitton at the end of 1988 and he saw the enthusiasm that I still had for the sport. He was pleased with the result on the Audi Rally and acknowledged that the rally programme could be used to promote the merger between Andrews and the newly-acquired Sykes Pumps. So he set out to use his negotiating skills to put together a high-profile two-car team. Ford provided the hardware, Mike Little prepared

Russell ran strongly in the Lancia on the 1987 RAC Rally, but sadly the challenge came to a premature end in Kielder.

Opposite: Russell, pictured on the Scottish Rally, made the most of the Sierra Cosworth's power and handling, despite the limitations of two-wheel drive. Consistent results gave him the runner-up spot in the 1989 Open Championship.

On the RAC Rally, unfortunately, I wasn't able to repeat the feat; I slid off on some ice, put a tree through the middle of the bonnet and had probably the hardest crash I've ever had. We got on the radio soon after the accident and spoke to the service crew:

'This is Oscar One to Oscar Service, come in.'

Jim Little replied, 'Oscar Service here.'

'Sorry Jim, we are out of the rally.'

There was a long pause, then Jim asked, 'What's the matter, what's the matter?'

'Broken the camshaft,' I said.

There was another long pause. 'Bloody hell, we've never broken one of those before. How do you know the camshaft is broken? You can't see it.'

'I can, I can see it sticking out of the tree!'

The six-month lay-off from rallying had given me a great opportunity to see if my heart was still in the sport,

the cars, Dunlop and Bristol Street Motors (at last) provided further support and I was joined by Mark Lovell to tackle the British Open Championship in 1989.

Right at the outset we realised it would be a difficult job. In theory, David Llewellin should win the forest rallies in the four-wheel drive Toyota, and the scoring system of the series, whereby only the best five scores out of seven were counted, effectively meant that David only had to do a four-round forest series with one additional tarmac event thrown in. Against that, we hoped to capitalize on the Sierra's reliability and anticipated that Llewellin would retire on maybe one forest round. That was the theory!

Owing to the fact that Phil Collins did a superb job on preparing the Toyota, and the team had luck run their way on occasions, they were able to win every forest round, whereas our plan fell apart on the Ulster Rally.

Mark Lovell, seen here on the Scottish Rally, received Andrews support during 1989 and played the part of Russell's team mate for the season.

On the 1989 Ulster Rally, Russell's strong challenge was curtailed by turbo failure, leaving victory to Gwyndaf Evans.

Cosworth on the 1989 Welsh Rally: Russell kept David Llewellin's Toyota under pressure all the way.

Powering out of a hairpin on the Ulster Rally under the watchful eye of a camera crew, en route to second place despite the turbo problem.

Russell and Berliner Peter Diekmann (right) celebrate their second place on the 1989 Circuit of Ireland Rally.

Hard at work on the 1989 Welsh Rally, an effort rewarded by second place. Andrews' signwriting was adjusted to suit the language of the host country, a nice touch.

The V6-powered Sierra XR4x4, though less powerful than the Cosworth version, provided a useful transition to four-wheel-drive. The 1990 Scottish Rally was Russell's third outing in the car and he finished third overall.

I had turned in all the performances expected of me during the year, but the car's turbocharger failed within two stages of the end, whilst I was in the lead. Although we managed to stagger through and replace the unit, Gwyndaf Evans got his nose in front and snatched victory, with me finishing second. This still took the series all the way down to the line and the Manx and Audi results became absolutely crucial.

The Manx produced a lot of heartache for me. My team-mate Mark Lovell had been placed in an exceptionally difficult position by Ford: a few weeks before, Ford's Competition Manager, Peter Ashcroft, had pointed out to him that Robert Droogmans was doing the event and stood to win the European Championship with a good result, and that Jimmy McRae, Gwyndaf Evans and myself had a chance of winning the Open Championship. Therefore, Mark was told that, should the need arise, he might have to finish fifth overall! In hindsight, I think that was a tremendously demoralizing thing to do to him.

Andrew Fitton saw his role as being to boost Mark's confidence. At that time there was a feeling around that Mark was the young challenger and I was being set up as the Aunt Sally, so I think that some people would have been happy to see him win the event. Nevertheless, we had put ourselves in a position to be able to challenge for the title and it was our results which were critical. I also think that Andrew Fitton resented the intrusion by Ford

into the running of the Andrews Sykes team.

We were leading at the end of the first day, with more than a minute's advantage over Jimmy McRae who held third place and a 16-second lead over Mark. It was then that Andrew Fitton told me of his game-plan: he would be quite happy if Mark charged ahead over the next two days, earning some publicity for himself and the team, and I was in no way to jeopardize the ultimate result by chasing recklessly after him. I was told that things would be put to rights on the last day if necessary.

We therefore started the second day in a difficult position, because if we pressed on and made a mistake we could only lose, bearing in mind that a good result was already decided for us. No one had told Mark in any detail what was going on and I feel that the game-plan backfired as he over-played the part and made it all very obvious when he had to hand back the lead. Few people saw further than the superficial situation – but it did produce more stories and publicity than the British Open had seen for a long time.

So the final round, the Audi Rally, was a do-or-die attempt to take my third British Championship. There was only one result which could ever count and that was to win, with David Llewellin being pushed into making a mistake and finishing lower than fourth. On the first four stages we almost achieved our goal – with a two-wheel drive car – until a spin threw my chance out of the window and gave David the title.

The Ford Sierra Cosworth 4x4 was the exciting new hope for the early 1990s. Russell and Neil Wilson took it to victory on the 1990 Manx Rally, giving the car its first international win and Russell his fourth on the event, matching Tony Pond's record.

But the year finished on a happier note, as I was reunited with John Brown to tackle the Rally of the Lakes, in Killarney. After ten years away from the hot seat, John was rusty at first, and we finished more than one stage with a page or so of pace notes still to be read. He soon acclimatized, however, we won the event comfortably and Andrews Sykes won the Irish Tarmac Championship in what was possibly the last appearance of a rally car in the traditional Andrews Heat for Hire colours.

As far as future plans were concerned, things went from bad to worse on the negotiating front. Andrew Fitton wanted to continue with a large, two-car team, but Ford weren't prepared to go along with it, as they wanted to concentrate wholly on their own preparations for the World Rally Championship with the new Sapphire Cosworth 4x4. What started out as being very promising for 1990, with Malcolm Wilson being introduced to the team, ended with Malcolm taking a works contract and Ford dragging their heels over support for Andrews even though there had been an expressed intent to be involved for two years. The whole package came to nothing in February, a sad end to an ambitious project which did much to put some sparkle into British rallying at a time when it desperately needed it. In the long term, I think that it will be seen as a wasted opportunity.

Things were very bleak and I had nothing to look forward to. It was clear to me that the four-wheel-drive Sierra/Sapphire Cosworth would surely be one of the most competitive cars around, and I felt that you had to be with a team which had the ability to get the car sorted and into action quickly. It was when these feelings were in my mind that Geoff Fielding of R-E-D came into the picture and put forward a proposal to run a 2.9i Sierra XR4x4, the V6-powered car, on the Open series. He felt that it would be a good test-bed for me to get used to four-wheel drive and for them in developing the suspension and transmission ready for the new car which would not be homologated until the second half of the year.

Neil's view was that we should contest only the forest rounds of the championship, because in Dunlop we had the most competitive tyre for gravel rallying and so that would be the best way to capitalize on the resources at our disposal. Peter Webber, the new Managing Director of Andrews Sykes, confirmed personal support for 1990 and the money for the car was provided by John Andrews, with major support from Texaco.

Finances were extremely tight but Geoff Fielding, to his credit, felt that unless we actually got the programme up and running we would lose credibility. We entered the Cartel Rally without the money to pay the bills and Geoff underwrote the project, but he made it very clear that we would need to acquire the necessary money within a few weeks of the event.

The car was not finished until the evening before scrutineering and consequently it was under-developed in certain areas. The engine management system failed in the Boltby stage and the car refused to start for five minutes. This put us out of contention for a top-three place, but we managed to fight back to fourth overall.

The Welsh Rally assault came to an end after a puncture-induced differential failure, but we went on to tackle the Scottish, where I'm confident that with a few more horsepower we could have challenged for a win. At the end of the two-day rally we were satisfied with third place overall.

We then moved on to the new Ford Sierra Cosworth

Russell in 1990. The advent of the Ford Cosworth 4x4, a really competitive car at last, brought a renewed sense of purpose and enthusiasm.

4x4, which was a totally different machine and offered well over 300bhp. The expertise of R-E-D really came to the fore at this time, because we had a lot of problems with the supply of components prior to the Manx Rally, the proposed debut for the machine.

Earlier in the year Ray Sherratt, the engineer at R-E-D, had asked me which gearbox we should use. He reckoned that the MS90 seven-speed unit would possibly introduce an element of unreliability and was too heavy as well as too complex. We opted for the five-speed 'Sport' gearbox and this proved to be a very wise decision. We made a number of small changes throughout the specification, but the biggest problem we encountered was a slight misfire which only occurred on severe jumps and bumpy terrain. Try as we might, we couldn't find the root of the problem: the mechanics changed the pick-up point for the fuel pipe, the fuel regulator, the fuel rail, the injectors, the distributor, the relays and the ignition pack, all to no avail. The circumstances which caused it were very difficult to reproduce and so the misfire remained a mystery.

Despite this problem we managed to tail the leader, Bertie Fisher, throughout the rally. Five stages from the end he collected a puncture on a road section, arriving at the next stage start in a fluster and changing the stricken wheel. I think the tension got to him, because the BMW went off on the next stage and Bertie collected a second flat tyre. Unfortunately on this event the battle wasn't confined to the stages alone, and Bertie, with the encouragement of other competitors, lodged a protest on the strange grounds that we had refused a stage start. The start marshal of the test in question was adamant that this was not the case, and we were pleased that the whole episode came to nought, enabling us to give the Ford

Night scene on the RAC Rally: adverse circumstances, including an errant service barge, interrupted a promising run.

Sierra Cosworth 4x4 its first international win, our first with Texaco.

The next event was the Audi Sport International which was our first forest rally with the car and so was treated as a development exercise, but I was very pleased to give the team its second win in a row. The experience was useful because we were able to refine the handling and identify an engine problem which had dogged us since the Manx. Small changes to the engine management programme transformed the car and so we looked forward to the RAC Rally, the big event of the year, full of confidence.

In 1990, for the first time, we were allowed to make pace notes on all the stages of the rally. I view the change with some regret, for although I am by no means against pace notes, I feel that the 'secret-route' format was an integral part of the RAC Rally and added to its appeal as an event with its own special character, not just another standardized 'Euro-Forest' rally. It also transformed the RAC from one of the cheapest World Championship events for participants to one of the more expensive ones.

Neil Wilson was unable to join me for the recce, as he was in the process of a major business transaction, so his place was filled by Ian Marshall, from North Wales, a club competitor who, with Neil's guidance, did an admirable job as a note-taker. Perhaps the most important aspect of pace notes is timing, and it is essential that a co-driver composes the notes in such a way that he can get the timing perfect 'on the night'. This of course was a big worry, with Ian taking the notes which Neil was to read, so we recorded all the stages on video. At intervals during the recce, Neil collected the pace notes and the appropriate videos and was able to sit in his office and check the notes in between phone calls!

The car was on fine form and Terry Hoyle had come up with an excellent engine specification that corrected the earlier hole in the power curve to produce a smooth, responsive motor. The first day of the rally went really well. Although running at number 22 (FISA B-seeded

driver) meant that there was a lot of mud on the tarmac sections of the spectator stages by the time we got to them, I kept in close touch with the leaders and finished ninth overall.

The second day saw further improvements which raised me to seventh, but already the pace of Sainz and Kankkunen at the front of the field was outstanding. The event then seemed to fall apart for us after a bizarre incident on the public road when a large station-wagon service vehicle drove into the side of the pristine car, smashing two doors amongst other damage. Shortly after that the alternator failed in Dalby, so depleting the electrical supply that the ignition system refused to work properly, losing us a minute to the leaders. Then on Gale Rigg, I overdid a corner, careering into the undergrowth and breaking a lower suspension arm in the process. Spectators lifted the car back onto the road after about 20 minutes and, although we thought we were out of the rally, they then set about tying the bottom of the suspension strut to the chassis with a tow-rope! This amazing repair enabled us to complete the next two stages, albeit at a very low speed, and stay in the event in a lowly 112th place.

There is a great temptation to retire in circumstances like that, but we decided it would be good for the whole team to keep going, even if it did mean splitting up the service crews to cope both with us so far down the field and Colin McRae up amongst the leaders of the pack. Running so far down the order was an eye-opener as we saw how poor the road surface in the stages becomes with the passage of cars, but it was a pleasure to mix with the clubmen – there is a great camaraderie at the end of the field.

By the end I had recovered to 36th place. Finishing at all was a reward for everyone's persistence, though my thoughts were still on what might have been a third overall – but that's rallying, and I look forward eagerly now to the next event, the next challenge.

3

Ways and means

For the newcomer to rallying, picking a suitable starting point can be quite difficult. The diversity of activity to be found is a measure of the sport's health, of course, but it can be confusing. People tend to divide rallying into categories on a kind of league-table basis, with the general assumption that you start at the bottom and work your way up towards the top. I don't think the sport should necessarily be seen like that, because each branch of rallying provides its own particular pleasures, and it is best to tackle those sectors which give the most fun to the individual concerned.

My own early motorsport career is a case in point. I drifted around on the periphery of rallying for quite a time, trying my hand at navigating, marshalling and competing in autocross and club rallies, as that was the only way that I could afford to compete in the early days. When I did acquire a rally car I decided to concentrate on international rallies almost straight away. I obtained my international competition licence without actually driving in any club events. I can admit now that my licence was signed by the stewards on several occasions even though I had tackled the events as a navigator and not as a driver!

By the time of the 1968 RAC Rally I had an international licence and it was that side of rallying which I tackled for the next three years. My feeling in those days was that you got more rallying for your money by contesting events such as the Welsh, Scottish and RAC than you did from competing in club rallies, which to me seemed to be a closed circus. In many ways it was true, for this was the heyday of the *Motoring News* Rally Championship, with many established names involved; people like John Bloxham, Rob Lawrence and Jimmy Bullough. This struck me as an ultra-specialist sport and it failed to capture my interest, which had been triggered by stage rallying when I worked as a mechanic for Richard Hudson-Evans on international rallies.

It was only later, when Martin Holmes introduced me to road rallying, that I started to take an interest in this side of the sport. So contrary to what many people seem to regard as the standard procedure, I didn't as a matter of course start my career in the lanes. I came to the conclusion that not only was club rallying at *Motoring News* level more expensive per mile than taking part in international rallies, but the latter also provided me with a bigger challenge and placed more of an emphasis on the driver. This meant that you didn't need the fastest car to be in with a chance.

My experience makes me firmly believe that anyone starting out in the sport should look carefully at what they really want from rallying. Too few people nowadays, I think, actually sit down and consider which aspect of the sport will give them the greatest enjoyment.

The first thing is to consider in detail the categories available. Of course it is true that club events can provide pleasure without an enormous commitment of time. On the other hand, longer events can be cheaper in some ways: to achieve results, for example, on single-venue rallies (events which take place entirely at the same location) you will probably need a faster car because the rallies themselves are short and seconds become of paramount importance for success or failure.

Standards of car preparation are very important and it is in that area where many people fall down. They bolt together a car with the best engine and suspension they can think of, or afford, but without doing any testing and development. I suspect that the first time most club competitors drive their cars in earnest will be over the start ramp on the way to the first special stage. That way, you cannot hope to realize the car's full potential – or your own. Even a limited amount of testing, be it just on an airfield or down a remote farmyard, is worth hundreds of pounds of money spent on equipment, and is particularly essential in preparation for short events where everything has to be right instantly.

For similar reasons, I would recommend that a car should always be readied well before a rally. This is where championships present problems because they take up a lot of money without giving a newcomer the time between events to develop and prepare a vehicle properly. The time and cost elements can become very difficult to control, as the competitor tends to feel forced to press on and contest rallies which he wouldn't otherwise do. So I have always suggested that people avoid becoming too concerned with the championship idea at the outset: far better to concentrate on one event at a time, to begin with.

My feelings are that most club competitors could derive more enjoyment from contesting a European international rally than they do from tackling a series of British events. I suggest that instead of hurrying off every third or fourth weekend to contest a national or BTRDA rally, you spend a little more time and effort to prepare for one or two Continental rallies. The further afield you go, the more interesting the events will become, and it is well known that even club competitors can obtain quite a lot of support from event organizers for this sort of venture.

Many of these rallies could be combined with a holiday, and Eastern Europe, for example, is an area which offers first class deals for foreign competitors. I have had many offers to tackle such events in recent years and, although these organizers do not as yet have Western currencies at their disposal, their generosity is often quite outstanding. It is commonplace that you have a substantial part of your petrol paid for and you are able to take advantage of free accommodation. At the end of the day, two or three Continental rallies will provide far more satisfaction than you would derive from contesting entire club championships at home.

Apart from the immediate enjoyment and satisfaction, it does make sense too in terms of building up experience and developing your abilities in the longer term. Most people in British club rallying suffer not so much from a lack of machinery or knowhow but from the lack of opportunities to drive competitively for long distances. Most British rallies are relatively short, while European events tend to offer the maximum stage mileage as laid down by FISA. Hence foreign events offer more

Even after he had begun to compete in the Mexico championship and the *Motoring News* series, Russell continued to enter the home internationals in a Mini. This is the Blenheim stage on the 1972 RAC Rally.

competitive miles for your money.

If you accept that this is the route to take, then you already have an idea which car you will need, as it is not worth travelling great distances only to have the car break down. Above all, reliability is the most important factor and it is essential to prepare a machine to a lower state of tune than you would in the British Isles, with more attention to the use of well engineered components to enhance that element of dependability.

As far as rallying in Britain is concerned, there has always been an element of confusion over which championship offers the best grounding for success. There is no question that the BTRDA Gold Star series, which has included eight forest rallies for several years, offers the newcomer a first class introduction to the art of forest driving. On a more localized scale, the regional single and multi-venue rally championships have their advantages, but the BTRDA series is an ideal starting point and gives an individual the chance to compete against some of the best amateur drivers from other regions in either homologated or non-homologated machinery.

Many competitors have progressed by graduating from the BTRDA series to an assault on the British National Rally Championship, which is similar in structure to the Gold Star series but offers an increased stage mileage, a chance to use pace notes on one tarmac rally and the opportunity to compete against top privateers and semi-works teams. But I think it is worthy of note that whenever we have contested BTRDA events, perhaps by way of a test exercise, I have been pushed much harder than by the competitors in the National Championship. I have therefore felt for some time that the latter series is overestimated and I for one was not unhappy to see plans for its eventual demise announced at the end of 1990.

Even rally fans have often been unclear about the distinction between the National and Open Rally Championships: as a simple rule it is worth remembering that national events generally last for one day, while Open rounds can span up to three days and offer a mixture of gravel and tarmac surfaces in England, Scotland, Ireland, Wales, Eire and the Isle of Man. The other big difference is that Open Championship rounds have international status, as opposed to the national status of National rallies and the restricted status of the majority of BTRDA Gold Star and all single venue events.

For many years the Open Rally Championship has been Britain's premier rally series, but over the last couple of seasons interest has begun to wane and now the RAC MSA is to restructure the calendar in 1992. The proposal entails combining both the National and Open series in such a way as to offer competitors the chance to contest what can unambiguously be called 'The British Rally Championship'. It is hoped that this step will inject much needed interest into the sport at its top level, whilst still offering the clubman the chance to compete on a relatively low budget.

The budget is, after all, what determines many competitors' plans to a large extent. When people first

Martin Holmes partnered Russell during his early days and encouraged him to look for sponsorship.

enter rallies, few appreciate just how much cost is added by factors beyond merely the preparation of the car, items like hotel bills, entry fees. travel, petrol and so on. It must also be realized that practice events are consequently considerably more expensive than secret-route rallies. Whilst the RAC MSA now seems to be appreciating this fact and is introducing rules to try and tighten up events, it seems a pity that their own rally, the RAC International, should suffer from their own good advice. In 1990 the governing body introduced a format permitting pace notes, not wanted by most competitors, which raised costs enormously.

The rules of a championship can be designed to reduce costs and can direct competitors towards machinery which is inherently reliable and therefore cheaper to operate. The classic example of this was the Mexico Championship: the greatest benefit for many drivers at the time was not so much that everyone was involved in the competitive element, but that the cars themselves were essentially reliable in their standard form and were therefore incredibly cheap to run. In 1972 I tackled 27

Tarmac rallies are expensive because they often require extensive practice periods. Russell and John Brown in full flight in the RS2000.

rallies in the Brooklyn Mexico and at the end of the season those events had only cost the garage £1,500. The engine only delivered around 90bhp, yet the car had many parts in common with the more powerful Twin Cam version, and therefore none of the components was overstretched.

It was the Mexico series which really gave my career a big push, not just because of the awards which were on offer or the fact that you were driving against people on an equal basis, but because of the simple fact that in those two years I contested something like 50 rallies. At the end of this period the cockpit of my Mexico felt like a second home. People entering the series late on were at a big disadvantage, even if they had spent large sums of money blueprinting their engines, because Nigel Rockey, Will Sparrow, Tony Pond and myself were so familiar with our cars that it became second nature to drive quickly. Nobody was going to challenge us until they achieved a similar level of experience.

Nowadays there are few championships which specifically promote up-and-coming young rally drivers,

although one-make series such as the Peugeot GTI Rally Challenge, Lada Challenge and Skoda Trophy do make it possible for individuals to contest events relatively cheaply. There is the occasional quest for a future driver, the one run by the *Radio Times* being an example, but not enough to really attract vast numbers to the sport.

Anyone trying to pick future rally winners is faced with the problem of how to assess driver talent. In 1981 I was asked by David Eddlestone of Castrol to be one of the judges on the Castrol *TV Times* Rally Challenge. This was to be held in the Nant-y-Hwych special stage in Mid-Wales and a short list of 24 drivers had been drafted out, each of whom had been nominated by their local motor clubs. They came along in their own cars and the idea was that several judges were positioned at various points on the special stage to witness the contestants' performances. Marks were awarded according to technique and driving style and from those a final selection was to be made. I arrived late and was firmly told by John Taylor, the other judge, that he had whittled the list down to six and there was no point in wasting time considering the other

18 any longer. I took this with a pinch of salt and decided to watch the drivers in action myself, coming to the conclusion that the selected individuals had been chosen not because of their driving ability but because they were 'promotable'. I felt that the times they had set on the special stage were entirely down to the fact that they had the best cars.

The fastest individuals around the stage included John Brown, from the North-East, who had Björn Waldegaard's ex-works Escort which had been re-prepared by his own mechanics and was in immaculate condition. I drove the vehicle later in the day and reached the conclusion that it was one of the best Escorts I had ever driven. Another shortlisted contestant was Ian Tilke, who also drove a works-specification Ford Escort. It soon became apparent that these individuals were flattered by the competitiveness of their machinery. There were other drivers present who had talent which wasn't able to shine through because of the quality of their vehicles.

We then had to take the day a stage further to eliminate the variable car element. I argued the point firmly with the *TV Times* personnel and decided, in an attempt to further examine the drivers' abilities, to take my life in my hands and sit alongside them. This is something I will never do again!

The rides were exciting, to put it politely, and it was a good job that an incident in a small Datsun 1300 occurred at the end of the session as I don't think that I would have sat in another car. Despite our pleas for steady driving, I found myself strapped in as a passive witness to a roll down the side of the hill in Esgair Dafydd, as the poor driver left his braking too late – about 100 yards too late! With some of the other drivers we visited the undergrowth too often for my liking, as well.

The next step was to drive the cars myself to become familiar with how each individual machine performed. This was difficult because some of the vehicles did not have adjustable seats and I am somewhat shorter than average. But each driver agreed that I could drive his car and, where my size presented a problem, the driving seat was stacked up with pillows. I said that I would drive the cars at only about 75% performance level, but it would give me an idea how my times compared with theirs.

John Brown had recorded the fastest time around the stage – 2min 14sec – but I found that by driving the car very smoothly it was possible to record a time 13 seconds quicker. With some of the other drivers, on the other hand, it was difficult to get near their times and it was apparent that they were wringing the utmost from their machinery. We whittled the list down to a different six drivers, and then had to find a method of assessing skill and eliminating the performance element of the vehicles again.

We found a steep section of forest track and secretly placed a marshal on the side of the stage, opposite a cone which we had erected. The idea was that the drivers approached downhill, carried out a handbrake turn around the cone and drove back up the incline. We then analysed the times they recorded downhill, as compared

Rallying's a serious business – but there's not much point in doing it if you don't enjoy it.

with their uphill times, and were thus able to assess the individual performances. Where the times were fairly close, we assumed that the cars were fairly powerful and were able to drag themselves up the slope more quickly.

Using this technique, we selected the final three drivers. They were George Gass, who still competes on club rallies in Scotland, Andrew Wood, who went on to become a works driver for General Motors, and Mark Lovell. I was very proud that two out of three men I picked at very early stages in their careers both became works drivers.

Choosing a car and choosing a type of event, or series of events, are of course closely bound up together. In the case of a one-make championship, the two decisions come as one package. But your own personal reasons for taking up rallying will affect your choice of car to a degree. It is vital that you consider whether your main aim in participating is to win, to gain experience for later ventures, or merely to enjoy yourself.

Generally speaking, a relatively small number of models make up a very high proportion of the cars being used in club rallying. If you choose one which is well developed by the factory, you have the advantage that parts are readily available and the car is proven in competition. I would always recommend the Vauxhall Nova and the Peugeot 205 GTI to anyone interested in driving a homologated car. They are reasonably light, fairly easy on tyres and are relatively cheap to run once the initial outlay has been overcome.

Alternatively, if you are rallying for fun, it is reasonable to choose a vehicle which is different, but you have to accept the fact that an unusual car is more often than not more expensive to run. To run an unusual machine, engineering facilities may become necessary to enable you to make components and be entirely responsible for preparation work. It may well be that the car will be more susceptible to breakage and mechanical failure, as ready engineered and tested parts are not available. But then, to some people, the development work is half the fun.

A classic example of an unusual car which has achieved considerable success in club rallying in recent years is Andy Burton's Ferrari-engined Alfa Romeo. Not only is it a spectacular sight to watch on the stages, but Andy has been able to develop components himself and cut down the cost of using outside engineering facilities. The 308 GTB engine is well proven and in standard form is relatively cheap to maintain. If you opt for a similar car, make sure that you have the motivation and the experience to develop and machine your own parts, otherwise the project could prove to be very frustrating as well as expensive and time-consuming.

Anybody with ambitions must initially choose a car which is reliable, as it is a vital factor to gain as much experience as possible. It's not much use having a very fast car but never finishing a rally! The Darrian glassfibre sports car is a good example of a low-cost machine which is cheap to run, fun to drive and which is now emerging from the area of truly specialized machines, on the

Mark Lovell was picked out by Russell as one of the most promising drivers during the Castrol *TV Times* finals.

Andrew Wood (pictured in Russell's Andrews Manta on the 1986 Granite City Rally) progressed from the Castrol *TV Times* competition to become a works driver for GM.

The Chevette, here on its way to second place in an Esgair Dafydd Rallysprint in 1982, served Russell well because it was reliable as well as fast.

The Opel Manta 400 was a car made competitive by extensive factory development work. Russell in the Errochty stage on the 1984 Scottish Rally.

Basically simple and also much developed by the factory, the rear-wheel-drive Escort can still be seen playing its part in club events, though it is many years since it was a top international competitor. Speech House, RAC Rally 1976.

grounds that it is developed sufficiently to be reliable.

If you intend to tackle single-venue rallies, you must realize that the shortness of the events emphasizes the need for a well-sorted car, rather like a sprint vehicle. The driver, too, needs to be able to switch on at once. As the time you spend behind the wheel actually competing is so small, I recommend that you do find some way to practice beforehand, by taking the rally car to an old airfield or a quarry where you can acclimatize to driving the vehicle quickly. This would go a long way to helping you turn in a first class performance.

As I hope I have made clear, there are so many ways of going rallying that there is no infallible prescription. I can only really ask the would-be competitor again to consider which area of the sport will give him or her the most enjoyment. If you have aspirations to becoming a professional driver, there is only one golden rule and that is that you must be seen to have beaten established works drivers, firstly on individual stages, and then on rallies. I stress the order of importance quite deliberately, because if a driver doesn't have the sheer speed, demonstrated by individual stage times, any rally successes will only be achieved by default and that in itself doesn't earn a works drive.

To achieve those fastest stage times you also need the correct machinery and back-up team, and the experience to use them. Unless a driver is very wealthy, the opportunity to have someone pay you to go rallying in such cars will usually only arrive once, and therefore you need to make the most of your chance without wasting the opportunity. Over the next few years it will therefore be interesting to follow the careers of two young drivers who have taken different approaches to the problem.

The two concerned have in common the fact that they are sons of eminent rallying fathers, but they have taken different routes within the sport: they are Colin McRae and Matthew Clark. The former has been pushed to the forefront of rallying, and this has added pressures and

problems. Having a well known father has given Colin the introduction to works machinery very quickly but, equally, has placed him under pressure to do well and this has led to accidents.

Roger Clark has adopted a very different approach with his son; we don't yet know what capabilities Matthew has, because he has started in club rallying and is working his way through the national scene. His father deliberately decreed that Matthew must build his own car as far as possible, and must tackle events out of the limelight to build up a sound base of experience in all aspects of rallying. This will stand him in good stead later in his career when he gets his hands on, say, a Group N Ford Sierra Cosworth 4x4.

This also highlights the fact that Colin has done himself a considerable disservice by opting to drive left-hand-drive cars. With the best will in the world, if you have been brought up to drive right-hand-drive vehicles, your body and mind become so attuned to your position in the driving seat that it is very difficult to adjust. Stig Blomqvist shares my opinion that it takes at least a year of driving nothing but either left-hand drive or right-hand drive, and that includes road cars, to complete a successful transition from one to the other. I am convinced that some of the past accidents suffered by both Mark Lovell and Colin can be attributed to using left-hand-drive machinery. Certainly they have had fewer accidents in right-hand-drive machines.

It is hard to pick which approach will be the most successful at the end of the day. If Colin McRae does have the ability to make the top flight, then he has adopted a shorter route to reach that position. I can't help but feel that the route forwards will be fraught with a lot of problems, and that he has been fortunate because his expensive crashes have been paid for. Support will not be available indefinitely and it may be that if Colin had two or three years more experience, better use could have been made of his talents. Time will tell!

Personal preparation

4

I am fortunate to compete in a sport where you don't have to carry your own body weight or need to be thin. If you look at pictures of old racing drivers, people like Farina and Ascari, they were well built, burly individuals. In many ways that is not a bad thing for a rally driver either. Having said that, though, I do try to keep reasonably fit, especially as I get older: the sport may not be hyper-athletic but it does make some physical demands. If you are not endowed with a reasonable natural level of fitness and the ability to keep going for long periods, it would be difficult to become a rally driver. My fitness activities are restricted to swimming and jogging – although everyone tries to persuade me not to take part in the latter in case I wear out my knee joints as my legs are short enough already!

It wasn't until 1978 that I began to give any specific attention to fitness. I had never felt any problems on rallies until then and stamina didn't seem to be something that I lacked. Bearing in mind that so many cars these days have power steering, one is apt to forget that hanging on to the steering wheel of a Mk2 Escort or an Opel Manta for a five-day RAC Rally was quite a tiring exercise. There was the odd occasion when I did suffer from cramp during the night, but those instances were very rare and were quickly dispelled by keeping warm, massaging the affected muscles and taking a drink with a little salt content.

Rallying itself has changed quite dramatically in the 20 years I have been competing. The Gulf London Rally was the first international that I took part in, navigating for Roger Platt and doing some occasional driving. That event started in Manchester on Monday morning and ran all the way through to Thursday night, entailing four days and three nights out of bed with no rest halts whatsoever. It was really tiring and certainly stretched all the participants to the limit of their endurance. The rally had to be curtailed because of the number of accidents it caused on public roads, particularly involving service crews, whose van drivers would fall asleep at the wheel. I certainly had my share of hallucinations as I tried to press on during the night. It's amazing what a range of tricks the mind can play at such times, the most frequent for me being images of little men sitting on gate posts at the side of the road!

The RAC Rally was almost as arduous in those days. Usually, the first leg would last for three days and two nights without a rest halt, followed by a second section of a day, a night and a final day, all with the long hours of November darkness. None of today's events put such great emphasis on the stamina and fitness of the driver.

When I started to take an interest in fitness I was introduced to Bernard Thomas, the owner of Edgbaston Health Clinic, former physiotherapist to the England cricket team and still involved with Warwickshire County Cricket team in a similar role. He came with me on the 1979 Tour of Cumbria Rally to see what the sport of rallying entailed. After observing a rally driver in action he drew the conclusion that it was definitely nowhere near as arduous as sports such as skiing and gymnastics, in which he was also involved. He considered it rather similar to cricket in terms of the stamina and physique required.

Bernard then devised a training routine which revolved around arm and shoulder mobility exercises. There is a great temptation among drivers to do weight training, but his view was that, as we have to move our arms fast and frequently, heavy weight training was not necessary or desirable because it tended to slow arm movements to a degree. I have spent some time on a weekly basis at Edgbaston ever since. I can't prove that my performances in rallying have improved as a direct result, but I can say that I am driving as well, if not better, at the age of 45 as I was able to ten years ago.

The most important single attribute for a rally driver is

good eyesight, but after discussions with eye specialists I have discovered that there is very little that one can do to maintain this. Avoiding too much of the drink can go some way to assisting the cause as it doesn't pay to arrive at a rally red-eyed and hungover.

Having said that, a good session before an event can be quite a successful way of breaking the tension which builds up prior to the rally. Much as I wouldn't recommend heavy drinking, Mike Broad will well remember an instance in 1982 when a very light party before the RAC Rally developed into a good crack! We both arrived at the start line with thumping hangovers which, if nothing else, meant that we stopped worrying about the problems of the rally. In a peculiar way, that can be relaxing and right from the start of that event I had one of my best-ever drives on the RAC, in a Vauxhall Chevette!

I am sure, however, that the temptation is for one session to lead to another, and so on. It was noticeable during the early 1970s, when the sport was developing at an international level, that many became somewhat

addicted to the drink. Undoubtedly the lifestyle of the professional driver, suffering from boredom between brief spells of excitement, being away from home for long periods and living in hotels where alcohol is readily available, led many to over indulge. It is particularly noteworthy that Finns seem to divide themselves sharply between those who are teetotal and the PAs!

But eyesight is so important and I have been fortunate to be blessed with very good eyesight. I am surprised that many drivers have paid little attention to this aspect. Defective vision (usually astigmatism) can radically alter your driving performance, especially at night.

Jimmy McRae was always a very fast driver but we knew that, as soon as darkness came, what had been a close battle would swing in our favour by up to ten seconds a stage. Then on the 1986 Cyprus Rally Jimmy took the plunge and went to see an optician – I suspect because Mike Broad had been telling him what a bargain spectacles were in Cyprus, and being a good Scotsman, he couldn't resist the chance to save some money! The effect

At work in the Manta. Rallying may not be an athletic sport but it does demand good general fitness and a measure of stamina. Good seating is essential to avoid possible back injury, particularly over jumps (opposite).

Relaxation after concentration. Paul White, at the piano, and John Andrews celebrate victory on the 1979 Manx Rally.

Good eyesight and a good sense of balance are important – and well co-ordinated arm movements to apply the right amount of opposite lock!

Russell in determined mood. The ability to switch on and focus the concentration has come with practice.

was dramatic: on that event, and subsequently, Jimmy became a major threat at night as well as by day. Similarly, on the 1990 Manx Rally much play was made of Bertie Fisher's new spectacles and again his performance dramatically improved. Good eyesight is the most important element of a driver's physical constitution and must never be overlooked.

Another area where fitness comes into play is when things go wrong with the rally car during a special stage. It is amazing how much quicker it is possible to change a tyre when one is physically fit and how much better one is able to cope with those low periods during the middle of the night.

The common ailments amongst drivers are back and spinal problems. It is therefore worthwhile spending money on a seat that fits really well. The head restraint area should be high enough to stop any whiplash injuries in the event of an accident, but above all the seat should ensure the right posture. Many adopt a racing-type reclining seat position, and this eventually puts strain on

the spine. The seat should be very upright, with the angle between the cushion and the squab approaching 90 degrees. In this way jolts are taken vertically down the spine. The position of the steering wheel and the pedals should then be moved to achieve a good driving position.

Sensible eating on events is also critical and is something to be careful to remember. The old adage 'little and often' applies well, rather than having a large meal. It is worthwhile planning out eating stops to try and keep some regularity and consistency in eating habits. When we do a long event Neil Wilson always arranges a rough plan with the team motorhome. This lays out when we have main meals and light snacks, because the temptation is to overeat. The people in the motorhome obviously consider it their duty to provide food and, if their enthusiasm is too great, it is easy to find yourself having breakfast at eight in the morning, another meal at ten after a mere three stages of the rally and then another meal at twelve, and so on.

The ideal situation is to provide proper meals as nearly as possible at the usual time of day and also to plan the main food stops to coincide with either a rest halt or a long road section which gives ample time for food to be properly digested. The last thing you need is to eat a heavy meal, dive into a rally car, start a special stage immediately and expect to perform quickly.

In the late 1970s, with many teams contesting the British Championship, the competition spread to the team chuck wagons and, on an RAC Rally, Judy Clark and Pam Peters offered roast pheasant with all the trimmings from their vehicle. Paul Wignell of the David Sutton team then responded at the next service point and we rushed to their motorhome for Crêpes Suzettes. The rally started to be of secondary importance to the gastronomic tour. On another occasion, whilst I was on holiday in France, I watched one of the last Alpine rallies. At one of the service points the Citroën team, managed by Madame Cotton, had picnic tables neatly spread with gingham table cloths, best cutlery, everything just so – what style!

Diet is a complex subject, and not one I have studied in detail, but the dieticians will tell you that pasta is an ideal food, in that it has a slow breakdown rate and doesn't absorb blood sugars in the process of digestion, which makes you tired. Chocolate and extremely sweet foods are best avoided: like glucose tablets which participants in some sports use, their effect on blood sugar levels is too short-term to be useful in rallying and can even be counter-productive.

Similarly, it is difficult to know what drinks to recommend: there is a temptation to take large quantities of Sports Drinks and the like with added salts and sugars, but rallying is hardly arduous enough to demand these. Much more importance should be placed on improving one's general fitness, as this is the only reliable way to get through an event. It is well known that excessive quantities of coffee are detrimental to performance because it makes you jumpy and hyped up, while large

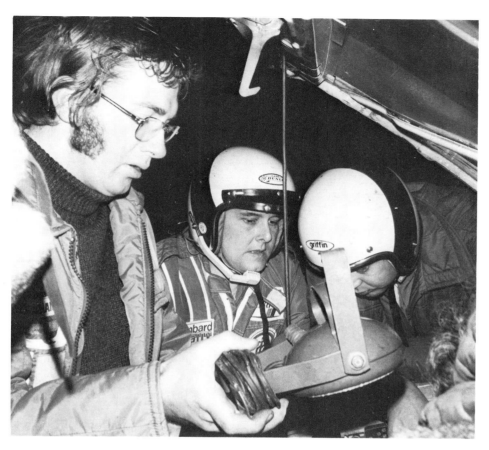

quantities of soft fizzy drinks are not recommended and certainly leave a cloying taste in the mouth after a time.

At the end of the day one comes to the conclusion that bottled water is the ideal drink. It quenches the thirst and replaces the body's lost water with no side effects. Dehydration is rarely a problem on today's shorter rallies, but rally cars do get very hot and in those circumstances dehydration can creep up on you. The effects are debilitating; the early sign is a hangover-like headache and the cure is to drink more water. Water has the advantage over all other beverages that if you drink it in excess the only problem is that you want to go to the toilet.

In very hot climates your water requirement can be quite extraordinary. The Cyprus Rally of 1986 took place in a heatwave with air temperatures up to 45 degrees Centigrade. The lack of ventilation in a Manta hardly made matters better, and I found that I was drinking about a litre of water at the end of each of the long stages.

Given a reasonable degree of fitness, there is no doubt that the most important factor in driving both fast and sensibly is the mental approach. What is needed can best be described as a delicate balance between adrenalin and coolness. From a personal point of view, I have often become too hyped up for my own good, although I rarely display it outwardly. In that state it is very rare that a driver can deliver a smooth performance and the tendency is to push too hard. As this occurs so your driving becomes

more ragged and the chances of accidents increase. It is almost as if there is a barrier which you can only occasionally force yourself through. Beyond that barrier there is a state of concentrated relaxation. I've noticed that when I drive really quickly it is almost as if my mind becomes detached from my body and I'm a third-party observer looking in at what I'm doing. At that point there seems to be all the time in the world to react to situations and cope with unexpected corners. This is a strange phenomenon which athletes also experience and which to me is like a state of euphoria. It is at that point that you not only realize you are driving at the maximum of your own ability, but you know that nobody else could drive more quickly in a similar car.

This is a great feeling but it is difficult to reach this level. The barrier can be broken through by an extremely hyped-up performance or through a step-by-step move up from a relaxed driving style. To achieve this state by the former path it is necessary to be a driver of exceptional ability and it is a route which will inevitably lead to accidents. A classic example of this was the late Henri Toivonen who was notoriously jumpy during rallies. In contrast, Walter Röhrl, for example, seemed to achieve a similar level of performance through the calculating approach. That method necessitates shutting oneself off from surrounding distractions and this is particularly difficult in modern rallying because stages are

Russell and Julia on their wedding day.

Wedding celebrations: Julia pushes the 'baby' in the Andrews-supported pushchair watched by John Andrews (right), John Brown, Mike Hill (centre), Auntie, Julia's sister-in-law and Peter Harrison.

relatively short – the longest time taken on a test nowadays is likely to be in the region of twenty minutes. At the end of that twenty-minute period it is vital to revert to a normal driving style and to traverse the public road at a pace which is not going to attract police attention. One then arrives at service points where there are the usual distractions of mechanics, journalists and spectators.

So rallying isn't just a matter of working oneself up to achieve the optimum performance on one stage, it is necessary to develop the technique of compartmentalizing the sport. For these reasons one almost needs a split personality. The rally driver must switch on at the start of a special stage and switch off at the end of the test. It is the latter which is often harder to achieve and I've noticed that some drivers shut themselves off from everybody's attention, keeping their conversation with mechanics and journalists to a minimum and hiding in the motorhome away from the public spotlight.

Personally, I find that I can switch into a mode where I will happily talk in generalizations to journalists whilst keeping a very firm barrier between what is happening inwardly in my mind and what the public sees. I think being able to do that comes from experience. All successful drivers have developed a technique of separating these distinct areas in the sport and a method of quickly switching between them. Without that ability it would be very difficult to concentrate fully on the special stages.

This split nature of rallying is something which still confuses the general public. Despite the publicity that rallying has achieved since the early 1980s, many people apparently still don't appreciate that the sport is divided into a number of short stages which are run against the clock and linked by road sections at normal speeds. Even now I have people asking me if I race all the way from Harrogate and back to Harrogate on an RAC Rally, and I am quizzed about the dangers to other road users. It is in this area where rallying is at its least understandable to the general public.

I never feel worried for either mine or my co-driver's safety when I contest a rally. If I ever started to feel concerned about having a crash, injuring the co-driver or hitting spectators, I just wouldn't drive quickly. It is something that doesn't enter my mind. I know that when I sit behind the wheel of a rally car I am in complete control. Unless you feel like that, there is no way that you will be able to drive really quickly. It is another aspect of

I met my wife, Julia, through my assistant at Land Rover, John Simpson, who was renting accommodation at Julia's mother's house: he told me of a girl who was keen on motorsport and wanted to meet Russell Brookes, the rally driver. He contrived a situation whereby I borrowed a record and took the opportunity of returning it personally, and that was when I met Julia and her family for the first time.

They were very welcoming and I was invited in for an excellent meal with the family and John. They say that the way to a man's heart is through his stomach and I think that Julia's mother certainly knew that. We had a very sumptuous coq au vin!

I took an immediate liking to Julia as she is very lively and has an extremely bubbly personality. She is very quick witted and excellent in company, although she is not necessarily a gregarious person when you get to know her. We hit it off very quickly, but I was surprised that the relationship survived as well early on, because we met in October, at the time when I was putting the finishing

The importance of a patient and understanding wife in professional rallying can never be underestimated. Julia (left) endures a joke with Stuart Turner and his wife.

needing the ability to compartmentalize your life.

The importance of the attitude of one's family cannot be overestimated when it comes to rallying or racing on a professional basis. These are extremely self-centred and selfish occupations and it is necessary to have a wife who can keep the home and children under control when you are away for long periods of time. This undoubtedly puts a strain on family relationships.

I noticed it particularly a few years ago when I contested longer events such as the Paris–Dakar, which necessitated being away for up to five weeks, and Corsica which entailed three weeks of practice. When I returned it was extremely difficult to settle into a normal family life again. To a degree I was a stranger in my own home and the children and my wife felt the same way, because they had become used to operating without me. It took a period of three or four days, even a week, to mesh back together again. If you are married it is very important to have a wife who can cope with this strain, being independent when required and adapting to married life when you come home.

touches to the car which we used for the 1975 RAC Rally, and Julia didn't see me again until after the event when she came to the prizegiving!

Our engagement lasted on into 1976 and we decided to tie the knot in July. Julia went through a period of finding out what rallying was all about and spent a fair amount of time manning the chuck wagons on events like the Scottish and Circuit of Ireland. She drew a lot of enjoyment from the sport and frequently travelled with John Brown's wife, Jo, and Pat Ridgway, the wife of one of my mechanics.

Travelling on events began to pale somewhat after a while, however, and once we had Robert, our first child, it was no longer possible for Julia to come out on rallies. I'm sure that she would agree that rallying isn't the sort of highly glamorous sport where you spend your life jetting off to exotic locations such as Monte Carlo or Rio de Janeiro – she would back me up when I say that Kielder, in the middle of winter, in the pouring rain, is not the most welcoming of places!

High spirits afloat: Anna and Robert.

I was not at home for Robert's birth and I think the vast majority of fathers don't realise what an important event the birth of your first child is. In retrospect I would have liked to have been present, but at the time I was away on the 1981 Circuit of Ireland Rally. Robert was born on April 17, which was a Good Friday that year, and also the day before the event started.

I telephoned the hospital frequently and was always put straight through to Julia every time. Only later did I realize that the nurses must have thought I was a serviceman away from home doing a tour of duty. I hadn't considered the implications of the fact that I was ringing from Northern Ireland! Robert was born at around 2.30 in the morning after a long labour for Julia. It was a very hard time, for it was necessary for her to have a Caesarean operation during the birth while I wasn't there and she was isolated during the trauma.

I remember next morning getting to the first stage, Ormeau Park, and the local interviewer for BBC Ulster Television came along with his microphone:

'Well, Russell, how's she going now?' he asked in his Ulster accent.

I said, 'Well, Julia's fine and Robert's fine, and . . .'

'I really meant the car,' he replied!

We had quite a good Circuit of Ireland in the Talbot and eventually finished third overall, albeit after the mother and father of crashes in front of Barrie Hinchliffe's cameras near the end of one stage where the caution boards for a sharp right over crest had been removed. We went sideways into a bank, but the best clip which appeared on television featured Mike Broad getting out of the car clutching his arm and swearing his head off. We managed to reach the end of the stage with three punctures, the chassis rail bent and one half of the suspension virtually ripped off. Jim Little did one of the most amazing repair jobs I have ever seen on a rally and we were able to continue just 20 minutes later, eventually to finish third overall.

We now have two charming children. Anna was born in 1985 and I was able to be involved in the event on this occasion. It isn't until you have your own children that you realize what tremendously interesting and complex characters they really are. It surprised me, not having had the experience of coming from a large family, how quickly children grow up. I naïvely thought that the baby stage would last for well over a year, whereas they are pretty mobile after nine months and begin to develop their own characters almost straight away. Alongside my wife, the children are the most important thing to me and their arrival certainly changed my outlook on life. Up until that point, rallying was very much all-consuming, but the birth of the children made me see that there was more to life than a sport.

5

Tyres and test sessions

Tyre choice is one of the most important factors governing the success of a top-level rally team, and has to be based on efficient tyre testing. It is vital to select a test venue which resembles the type of roads that you will be driving over. It is in this area where works teams have the biggest advantage, because good tarmac roads are very difficult to come by for testing and hiring a section of forest may cost up to £750 per day. At one time or another, many teams have resorted to using race circuits, which is an absolute waste of time. Even by taking a rally car to a twisty track like Cadwell Park you only end up with a car which is quick around that race circuit. As soon as you get it into the real stages you realize that it is no good at all. For Manx, Irish and other tarmac rallies the only place to go testing is either the Isle of Mull or Ireland itself which, for a private entrant, is a costly exercise.

Testing in Ireland has always been a practical proposition, though, because the number of cars on the roads in rural areas is so small. It is easy to select a piece of suitable deserted road and go out and test for up to three or four days. We have usually found it possible to block off the road unofficially when the car has a run: so long as you don't hold people up for more than a minute or so, nobody has ever objected in my experience. This is one of the welcoming and friendly aspects of the sport in Ireland. Mull is very similar, but on the UK mainland it is almost impossible to find suitable places to go testing. Undoubtedly the best place we have found is in Ireland – but I won't tell you where! At the end of a hot day's testing there is nothing better than to slip down a Guinness in Mrs Nugent's bar located just at the end of the test venue.

Every time we have been tyre testing, setting the car up accurately against the tyres, making sure the castor and camber angle are correct and studying the best rubber compounds for the conditions, we have come away with the machine being in the region of a second per mile

quicker. When you apply this, for example, to a Manx International Rally with 250 stage miles, a second a mile begins to look impressive, to say the least. In practice, it is very rarely that you experience the full benefit of a tyre test session on the rally, but certainly we usually expect a factor of 50%. Not only is this testing important to determine which tyres are correct, but of course it also provides the driver with vital training.

It is important to approach test sessions with an open mind. A knowledge of what each adjustment might do to a car is important, but it is equally vital not to have preconceived ideas as to what may or may not be the best. In many instances you have to be guided by the engineers and fall in line with what they want to try on the car. Sometimes, in fact, it is a good idea not to know what changes have been made.

The importance of this open-minded approach to a test session was brought home to me in 1988, when I took part in lengthy tyre test sessions in the forests with Dunlop, shortly before the Audi Rally which I eventually won, a victory in large part attributable to the work we put in during our testing beforehand. It has become common policy for teams to change tyres at every opportunity, the belief being that fresh tyres with a sharp cutting edge on the tread blocks are best. What we proved during those Dunlop tests was that this was not the case with their tyres: the performance at first improved slightly as the treads wore, then remained identical to the point where the tread blocks were completely worn away and the tyres were almost bald. Whereas we would always have changed the rears after about eight miles before, we proved that it was better to leave them on until they had done 18 to 20 miles, and that produced the fastest performance.

If we had tyres which had done 10 or 12 miles and we were faced with a 10-mile stage, we would take those

Even in the early 1970s tyres took a hammering on both tarmac and gravel stages. Russell is pictured at the wheel of the RS2000.

tyres off and refit them later for a shorter stage. In the first two-mile run on a test circuit, the car would record a time of, say, 2m 07s; the next run would give a time of 2m 06s, on the third run we would record 2m 05s, and the times would then stay absolutely constant until 18 miles, when they would begin to increase by about a second every lap until 22 or 24 miles. At this point the tyres were completely worn out and the times began to drop away dramatically. By fitting a second-hand tyre for a four-mile stage, we were actually going to be two or three seconds quicker than we would have been with new tyres. The lesson might not apply to other tyres or other conditions, but it was a valuable example of what could be learnt from careful testing.

It's clear, too, that consistent driving is vital: to achieve good results in test sessions it is important to drive not absolutely flat out, but very close to your quickest pace at a performance level which can be repeated time after time. Usually a test session begins with getting familiar with the section of road that you are going to use and I often drive over it eight or nine times in an ordinary road car just so that I know the road well before we start testing. The second thing is to avoid the problem of

variations in times due to erratic starts, especially on tarmac, and my policy is that we use rolling starts and always pass a fixed point at a certain number of revs in a certain gear. We never start testing proper until I am confident that I know the road fully and I'm sure that I can repeat a time to within one tenth of a second or so. Only at that point can serious testing really begin.

The first point is to establish the basic specification of the car, and the cardinal rule is that you only ever make one change at a time. If you alter two things, an element of doubt is immediately introduced as to which change actually made the difference. It is also critical to revert to the original specification after every dozen runs so that you can check whether you personally are driving quicker. If the time goes back to what it was before, you can say that you are driving the same as before. If the times differ, you can assume that you are driving harder, perhaps because you are more familiar with the stage in question, and it is then necessary to compensate for that in the calculations.

If we introduce a change which dramatically improves the car's performance, we then drive on this specification for a while before reverting to the original set-up, to

Tyre choice was important when Russell campaigned a powerful Opel Manta 400, seen here lifting a front wheel on a tarmac stage during 1984. Having the right tyres for the conditions was critical, for example, on the 1985 Circuit of Ireland.

confirm the time, and then fit the new specification again to ensure that it wasn't a change in my outlook on the stage which caused the improvement.

Because you do need to learn the test venue quickly, it is important to ensure that you don't choose somewhere which is too long and so takes too much time to learn. We tend to find that a stage between two and four miles is ideal for testing purposes, so long as it contains a good variety of corners of a type that you are going to come up against on a rally on which you will compete. The road should also have jumps and bumps, if they are a feature of the particular event you are planning for.

While familiarity with the test venue is essential, it can also cause problems. One of the commonest failings in testing occurs because when you become accustomed to a particular road, you are able to drive more quickly with stiffer suspension, which under other circumstances may make the car unforgiving and difficult to drive. It is always worth remembering that the car will have to be driven on a road that you don't know so intimately, even on pace notes. For this reason it is always worth slightly backing-off the suspension stiffness.

The relationship between suspension settings and handling is a complicated one, made up of many variable factors. For this reason, it is vital that tyre and suspension testing is carried out in harmony. As you become familar with the detailed characteristics of the car during testing it is possible to feel the difference made by tyres which have different internal construction. Traditionally, Pirelli tyres have very stiff sidewall structure, whereas Dunlop have soft sidewalls: consequently a change from one make to the other necessitates altering spring and damper rates. To optimize the performance of the tyre, each will also have different camber settings. The effective spring rates of the tyres are altered by a change in inflation pressure, and variations of 0.2 to 0.4 bar can have marked effects on the performance of the car.

Testing is made up of tedious detailed work of this

type, but at the end of the day it can produce quite dramatic results. If people involved in rallying at clubman level could ever arrange to go out and do even the simplest testing, they might well be surprised what can be achieved. The key to a successful test session, however, lies in the skill of the engineer. It requires, too, a worthwhile starting point: if the car is not basically sound, well prepared and close to the optimum specification, no amount of fiddling at the side of the road will transform it into a winner.

Particularly in two-wheel drive cars, traction in the forest is always at a premium but the most inconclusive test sessions were always when we tried to improve the traction. No matter how careful I was, it was impossible to achieve consistent standing starts and the times varied

enormously. I discussed the problem with Talbot engineer Maurice Millar and we came to the conclusion that whatever the times we achieved, an improvement in traction should result in less wheelspin and therefore fewer wheel revolutions for a given distance. It was then a relatively simple task to connect a Terratrip to the rear wheels and calibrate it to read off wheel revolutions, giving us a much more precise way of assessing the amount of slip.

On tarmac rallies, I always insist that the tyre vans carry one set of wide forest tyres, for use when the road is totally awash with rain. On the 1985 Circuit of Ireland Rally when I was having a battle with Jimmy McRae, there was an incredible downpour shortly after the Galway halt. The organizers had been forewarned of this

by the weather forecast and issued a bulletin at the halt to allow competitors to change tyres in what was otherwise a 'no service' area, before a group of stages beginning with Taylor's Hill. Jimmy fitted wet racing tyres, I fitted those wide forest tyres and on this one stage we took over a minute from him. It was almost an exact replica of what had taken place on the Circuit of Ireland Rally seven years previously.

I've experienced similar circumstances on Belgian rallies, too. The roads are very flat, with little drainage, and water often sits in hollows between fields with no ditches either side of them. If there is heavy rain, mud runs off the fields and water collects between the low banks, making the surface very slippery. The importance of forest tyres for those conditions was brought home to

the puncture risk. If the tarmac comes first I almost invariably choose a tarmac tyre, because if you sustain a puncture in the second half of the stage it won't be very time-consuming. If the start of the test is loose-surfaced then it is a toss-up whether you fit a tarmac tyre, because if you do get a puncture early on you can lose an enormous amount of time. If forest treads are the choice, it is very important to fit the widest possible tyre, particularly to the front of the car to reduce the amount of understeer on the tarmac section.

The subject of punctures reminds me of the 1983 RAC Rally which I tackled in a Vauxhall Chevette with Mike Broad. We were holding fifth place, ahead of Timo Salonen in the Nissan 240RS, nearly three minutes in front of him, but all the time concerned about picking up

me when Guy Colsoul used them to take an enormous amount of time out of us on the Haspengouw Rally. We learned the lesson and took some forest rubber for the same event the following year, and again they proved to be very useful when we had a heavy downpour. You should, however, drive on the tyres in a test session before the rally to find out how the car behaves.

It is always difficult to choose which tyre to use on a mixed-surface stage, a test which is part tarmac and part loose gravel. The tendency nowadays, however, is for organizers to shy away from using such tests. Experience tells me that on a test which is 50% loose and 50% tarmac, a racing tyre is always a lot quicker so long as there is no deep mud about which makes driving on racers very difficult. But tarmac tyres are much more easily punctured, so I always try to make an assessment of

a puncture. In fact we became a bit paranoid about it. In the middle of a Dyfi stage I slid sideways into a corner and collected an enormous clod of mud in a rear wheel. My immediate reaction was that we had a puncture, as the axle started to tramp very badly and the car slowed down with the rear wheel spinning off the ground half the time. I arranged with Mike Broad to do a wheel change and he readied the wheel brace. It was then a matter of finding a suitable place – on a night stage – where we could pull over and change the wheel. Eventually we found a junction where there were several marshals. As we stopped and jumped out of the car they switched on their car headlights to see what was happening and floodlit the whole area. They then witnessed myself taking the jack out of the boot and rushing to the left-hand rear tyre, which was the one I thought was punctured, in time to meet Mike

Corsican memories: Jean-Pierre Nicolas, nicknamed Jumbo, top rallyist and gastronome.

head-on coming the other way. We both proceeded to fall over and there was a heated exchange of words.

We ran all round the car, only to find all four tyres properly inflated. In the light of the torch I saw the mud which had now dropped out of the wheel, and Mike and I leapt back into the Chevette and continued down the stage. I never discovered what the marshals on that particular corner thought about the antics they'd witnessed!

Punctures are always a problem in rallying, although very few crews ever practise tyre and wheel changes prior to events. It is essential that the equipment needed to change a wheel is close at hand and that the driver and co-driver adopt a set procedure. Ideally, the driver should be back in the seat, strapped in, helmet on, intercom connected, with the engine running, at the very moment

that the co-driver finishes.

It is vital that you make up your mind quickly whether it is necessary to change a wheel. It is possible to drive for a maximum of three or four miles with a puncture on tarmac, and six or seven in the forests, but you must assess the level of damage that the car may sustain should you decide not to change the wheel. If the puncture is on the driven axle, continuing to drive will overheat the differential and increase wear in the limited-slip mechanism. It is also possible to damage the shock absorbers and risk irreparable damage to brake pipes and calipers. All these factors have to be taken into account.

If the decision is to go for the wheel-change, it is vital to find a level piece of ground, at least to one side of the road for safety reasons, where the jack will not sink into mud or damp grass. Normally we adopt the system whereby the co-driver gets out of the car and releases the wheel nuts, while I remove the jack and spare wheel from the boot and raise the car, by which time the co-driver has the nuts loosened. The wheels are then changed, I put the spare in the boot if it is worth saving, and he will tighten the nuts while I return to my seat and start the engine. He tends to arrive in a big heap with the jack in his arms, in time to watch me speed off down the special stage. The objective is to try and get away before the second car appears, assuming that competitors commenced the stage at the usual one minute intervals.

Undoubtedly one of the best test sessions ever was in Corsica with Ford and Jean-Pierre Nicolas (nicknamed Jumbo). Testing on the island is reminiscent of a large party: although the mountain roads are very remote, it seems that you only have to be there ten minutes and crowds of spectators arrive, bonfires are lit and the barbecues start. Jumbo's culinary speciality was sea urchins and at every test session he would arrange for friends to supply crates of these black, spiny creatures. A special pair of cucumber scissors would be produced and in between runs he would tuck into the slivers of orange flesh. I tried sitting in with him for a few runs, but the combination of sea urchins and the co-driver's seat soon made my stomach cry enough!

I have, during various test sessions, had the opportunity of sitting alongside other drivers as well – people like Hannu Mikkola, Markku Alèn and Mikael Ericsson. Every time, I say to myself I will never do it again, as I find myself petrified, car sick and thinking 'I could never drive that quickly!' which is very discouraging, even though you realize how different is the view from the co-driver's seat. I don't know how or why co-drivers do their job, but I can understand why so many of the professionals are short-sighted – they can't see what's coming!

6

Partnership in success

The role of the co-driver is particularly varied. I'm always surprised how little this position has been exploited in rallying. The sport is almost unique in the sense that there are very few other sports where you have somebody sitting alongside experiencing first-hand what is going on and yet not directly involved in the physical activity and so in a position to give advice or help in some way. The nearest I can think of to this situation is a caddy in golf. Many golfers say that they turn in better performances with one caddy than with another. It is extremely difficult to define why that should be, but certainly the standard explanations don't seem true, to my mind.

Very often, it seems that most co-drivers regard their role as one of whipping up the driver to make him go faster. My experience suggests that this is very rarely what is required. It is usually a much more subtle and gentle approach that is needed in terms of generating speed – if anything is required at all.

I have always been surprised that no co-driver has ever set himself up as 'the professional mentor', like the coach in other sports. In tennis and golf you have people who follow players' careers very closely and watch every aspect of their play, from swings or serves to diet and attitude. In rallying we have the ideal opportunity to do a similar thing, because a top co-driver may have sat alongside many of the world's greatest drivers and is therefore in a position to pass on very valuable experience. This has never been done on a professional basis, and I feel that a good co-driver could hire a test venue, acquire a good reliable car and hire out his services to people in need of tuition in driving techniques, or provide his services to paying amateurs on rallies.

It is important to recognize, even before you team up with a co-driver, that the requirements are probably very different for an amateur than they are when you reach a professional standard. But whatever the level, the aspect which is so important in the co-driving world is accuracy, in that drivers win rallies but co-drivers lose them. He or she can very rarely affect the result of a rally in terms of creating a win, but an inaccurate co-driver, who gets you lost or books you into a time control early, instantly throws away an event for you. Rallies have to be run to time schedules, and it is vital that you have a co-driver who is meticulously careful in his time keeping.

When you start out in the sport, the role of the co-driver is very often one of partnership, a friend to have alongside in the car. Particularly in club rallying it is often someone who helps pay the way and someone to share the fun with – as well as navigate. The importance of this companionship should not be underestimated. But when you are competing on more than just a casual level then it is time to look at his/her other attributes.

The most careful person I've ever been with must be Mike Broad. In our seven years of rallying together he never made a significant mistake of any kind whatsoever, certainly not in time-keeping and never significantly in terms of navigating. My early co-drivers were people mainly found by placing adverts in *Motoring News*. These were people with whom I generally had good fun, and I was very fortunate in that I also picked people who rarely made big blunders. In many ways, this was a very good introduction to the sport for me.

A classic example of someone who has worked hard and matured way beyond the level of ability he had in his earlier career, and who did make the big blunder, is Kevin Gormley. We did the Sherry Rally together in 1971. It was a very long and arduous event and it came to a point where I said that I was too tired to drive any further. We had begun a relatively long road section and Kevin took over the driving. Eventually he decided that he was too tired to continue and stopped in a lay-by for a few minutes 'shut-eye'. The problem was that I woke up twenty minutes later to find Kevin fast asleep in the driver's seat and us miles over the time schedule!

All my regular co-drivers have been significant in terms of steps forwards in my rallying career. Martin Holmes was very important: although he is now a very respected motoring journalist, I think he is at heart a frustrated competitor who would dearly have loved to have been recognized as one of the world's top co-drivers. Yet I feel Martin lacks a little spark which is needed to motivate drivers. He is more of an observer than a participant, which is probably why he is such a good journalist. He taught me an enormous amount about preparation and presentation. It was Martin who introduced me to the world of sponsorship, showing me how to produce good press releases and undertake proper

presentations, and how to treat sponsors properly. He introduced a level of professionalism at an early stage, which I've tried to maintain ever since.

In many ways that was a critical lesson in terms of enabling me to stay in the sport for so long. Rallying is very expensive and, at the end of the day, you can only compete if someone is prepared to give you a drive or if you are fortunate enough to raise the necessary sponsorship. That is only achieved through professionalism.

The next co-driver I had was John Brown. Over a lengthy association I learned a great deal from John, both on the positive side and, in a few areas, on the negative. John is intensely competitive and his burning desire above all was to win. To a large extent, he instilled those beliefs into me, and it was with John that I won my first rally. Even though the Taunton Rally was only a club event, it made me realize that anything other than winning didn't really matter after that.

It was with John that I won the first quarterly award in the Mexico Championship and then went on to contest the Jim Clark Rally. On that event I began to believe that I could drive a works car faster than other people. I learned the spirit of competitiveness, the idea that you must keep going when others are flagging, the belief that then is the time to commence a charge. In the middle of the night, in the pouring rain and when everything seemed to be going wrong, it was John who really taught me that if I wanted to take time off people, then was the time to attack. I learned the art of picking the difficult stages to attack on, the ones that most other competitors shy away from.

John, rather like many of the old school of co-drivers, was also a great believer that he could radically influence the performance of drivers by whipping them up and making them drive quicker. In some cases it can be productive, but at other times it may have an adverse effect. It wasn't until recently that I had a co-driver who could show that a similar performance could be achieved through other means. Obviously, though, unless the driver has talent in the first place, there is no way that a co-driver can help – you can't make a silk purse out of a sow's ear!

I remember one of John's early little tricks on long stages was to start looking over his shoulder. The immediate reaction is that someone is closing behind and you begin to drive faster. On a very foggy RAC Rally one year, John Brown was co-driving for John Buffum, using his local knowledge and map reading ability in Yorkshire to get Buffum to drive flat-out up and down the Langdale straights in pea-soup fog. At the service point, when we were alongside their TR8 in a Ford, Buffum clambered out of the car. In his broad American accent, he shouted out to all concerned, 'Gee, that man is no respecter of

human life!' In a sense that illustrated John Brown's failing – he didn't always appreciate when the time came to ease off. To this day I don't know if it was connected or not, but later in the event Buffum retired 300 yards up a firebreak!

Certainly there were times when John pushed too hard, and we had quite a few accidents. His attitude created tension in the car which could be counter-productive. Some of my best drives came after we'd had an accident or a mechanical problem. On the 1977 Scottish Rally we had the distributor break on the Errochty stage. We managed to push the car for four and a half miles out of the test and carried out emergency repairs. Pushing a car on a loose surface is the next best thing to having a heart attack. All credit is due to John, as we managed to do it, and then went on to take 22 fastest times in a row. At times like that, the immediate reaction of an outsider is that something has happened to get me fired up when, in fact, the incident had broken the tension that had been created by the rally. I was able to relax and get on with the job without having to compare my performances with other people. I don't feel that John fully appreciated this fact.

There are several little tricks which co-drivers use in an attempt to speed up the driver. In addition to looking over their shoulders to see if a car is closing from behind, another favourite is to play absolutely cool and look out of the window at the scenery to try and convey the impression that you are not actually driving quick enough to worry them.

There are also various methods of seeking revenge on a co-driver. The classic is to leave the start ramp of the rally and, if everyone else turns right, turn left in front of all the spectators! That really upsets the co-driver! A subtle method can be applied when you are well into the rally: you come out of a special stage and drive down the road, where there may be a few service vehicles, spectators or even journalists around – it's always best

Russell and John Brown press on towards success in the Mexico Championship.

when there is an assembled gathering of press folk! Then, at a T-junction where you should turn left, you put the right-hand indicator on and pull to the right-hand side of the road, by which time you have the co-driver screaming at you to turn left. You then grab the road book from the co-driver and hold it up in the air as if you are examining it. This ensures that everyone spectating on the junction can see that the co-driver is unsure of his way. The ruse is completed by throwing the road book back at the co-driver, signalling left and turning left!

At one period, I was accompanied by a series of different co-drivers in quite rapid succession. Paul White sat alongside in 1979 and Peter Bryant did likewise in 1980. Peter Bryant was absolutely in the John Brown mould, because of his burning desire to win. He was keen to extract the most from me and would push me and the regulations to the limit to achieve his goals. Peter then became more involved with his business and I began to rally with Mike Broad.

We had a very long and happy association. Mike was technically perfect, in that he never made mistakes and he always did absolutely what the driver wanted from him. In some ways, our partnership went on too long and what we really wanted was a break. That is effectively what happened in 1988 when I took six months off from rallying.

This could have been a natural lead-in to calling it a day and dropping out of the sport, but I suddenly realized that I really missed the scene and wanted to continue and win rallies. That short break did me a lot of good and I've driven very well since my return. Part of the credit, I'm sure, must go to Neil Wilson.

Neil is one of the most experienced co-drivers in Britain today. He has contested fifty American Championship rallies, twenty-five to thirty European Championship events, he won the RAC Rally with Henri Toivonen and he has been associated with many works teams. But he doesn't always get the credit that he deserves. He has co-driven for people like Ari Vatanen, Hannu Mikkola and Roger Clark, and gained vital experience on the way.

He takes a very different view of the co-driver's role from the traditional one. When necessary he will encourage the driver to go faster, and he can read the maps very well, but he is also aware of the limitations of a co-driver. I find that map reading is only successful if it is as accurate and as reliable as pace notes. Only then can I totally commit myself to what the co-driver is saying. If, as so often happens, maps are not accurate enough to be read in that way, co-drivers end up giving vague instructions. In my view that is the best way to slow a driver down, because it raises a degree of uncertainty in the driver's mind about what is coming up next. If you know that there is a sharp corner in the next quarter of a mile you are always on the look out for it and you slow for corners unnecessarily. If a co-driver is to read anything to me it must be totally accurate.

The other thing that Neil appreciates is that a driver only performs at his optimum if he is relaxed. He is extremely good at defusing and relaxing situations. He is excellent at reading what other competitors may be thinking at a given time, and therefore understanding the strategy needed to win rallies.

Neil has become very important in my driving. As with all co-drivers there is never much tangible that you can put down to your relationship with them, but Neil has this ability to create a good atmosphere in the car. Driving a less competitive car in the British scene for the last two years, we have managed to turn in performances

Opposite, left to right: Peter Bryant, John Brown, and Ronan Morgan.

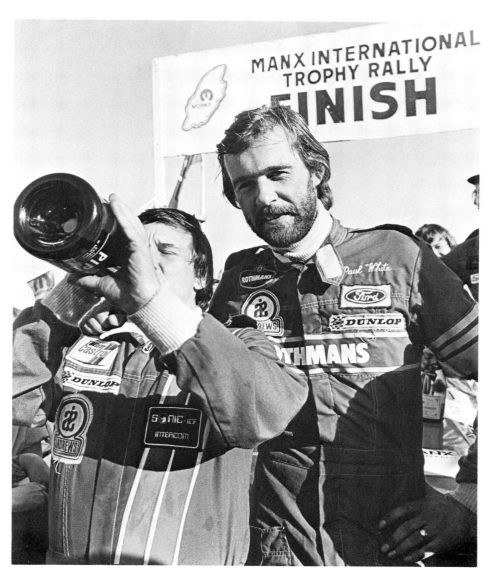

Partnership in success: Russell and Paul White celebrate victory on the 1979 Manx International Trophy Rally.

which were well beyond expectation and in large part I put that down to Neil's abilities in recognizing the circumstances in which that kind of result can be created. Each co-driver I've had has brought out one special attribute in my driving, but Neil is probably the best all-round co-driver I've ever been with.

Over the years, I have contested several events with Derek Tucker. Our relationship began in the days of road rallying, where we had an very successful run, initially winning the Virgo Galaxy in 1972 and then the Targa Rusticana. Derek came back into the picture in 1978 after the split with John Brown, when I also took Peter Bryant on selected rallies.

We tackled the RAC together that year under very difficult circumstances. Shortly before the rally I'd been playing squash with a friend who miss-hit the ball and, although I was wearing eye protectors, the ball skimmed across my eye and caused a haemorrhage in the retina,

which, in turn, created blood clots in the aqueous humour. I can still see their outline, which makes it very difficult to drive quickly in fog, as the clots are more visible when I look at a really plain background. The eye was still very painful and for large sections of the rally I resorted to wearing a patch but, despite my being christened Long John Silver, we finished third overall. In Wales, Derek decided to play the local marshals' patriotism:

'Give us five seconds for a Welshman, Boyo,' he'd say at the start line. I was quite amazed at the number of stages where we did sneak the odd few seconds, especially bearing in mind that Derek might be an adopted Welshman, but he actually originates from Somerset!

I have had many other co-drivers during my career. In 1980 I tackled the South East Asian Rally Championship. Peter Ashcroft had been approached by the Ford Dealers in South East Asia and I was asked to drive an Escort in the series. I wanted to arrange for Peter Bryant to tackle the

rallies with me, but they refused on the grounds that they had a perfectly good co-driver of their own – Mr Ho Puay Koon! He was introduced as the All-Malaysian Champion and in effect the 'greatest thing since sliced bread'. Rather like with locally-built cars, you tend to assume that the general standards leave a lot to be desired in European terms. I stood my ground on the decision for a while, but eventually they refused to pay the air ticket for a British co-driver and I was left with no alternative but to use the local man. I was also worried because of the possible language difficulties. The one thing in his favour was that he was a manager at the Guinness brewery in Kuala Lumpur!

I soon changed my views very rapidly, however. Upon arrival at the airport I was taken to the Ford dealership to look at the car, an Escort RS2000 built to Group 1 specification without the large wheel arches. It looked to be quite well prepared. The most noticeable thing was this enormous chain-saw bolted down across the back parcel shelf, where I was normally accustomed to finding

a tool roll. I enquired why it was in the car and was very firmly told that it was to be used to cut through the trees that might have fallen on to the road. When I questioned how likely that was on special stages, I was told that it was a distinct possibility! I asked if there was a course car which went through the stages before the competitors and was told that there wasn't. We were seeded at number two on the rally so I told the assembled gathering that I felt it rather harsh that if there were trees in the way on the route other people would benefit, after we had spent time creating a free passage. 'That is why we have given you a *big* chain-saw,' quipped a local!

I had still not been introduced to my co-driver when I visited the dealership the following day. While I was talking to the workshop foreman I noticed a very studious Chinese gentleman kneeling in front of the car doing something or other. I watched him carefully out of the corner of my eye as I talked to the foreman. This man had a piece of string on the floor, which he cut up and

Opposite: Russell and Mike Broad during the Vauxhall years.

Austin Frazer (front left) congratulates Bertie Fisher (front right), while Russell (back left) and Mike Broad (back right) celebrate victory on the 1983 Circuit of Ireland Rally.

wrapped in tape before sticking it on the inside of his door pocket. We went over to the man and I was introduced to Mr Ho Puay Koon.

We chatted about things and eventually people drifted away and I took the opportunity to speak to him. I questioned him about the need for a piece of string and, in his best Chinese accent, he replied, 'Ah, RS2000 Group 1, very narrow car, do not have big wheel arches, piece of string measure width of car. If we cut hole through trees we only make hole big enough for our car to go through. Other cars cannot go through!'

At that moment I realized that this man had something special about him. In fact, I also took him on an event in the Philippines and he turned out to be one of the most efficient co-drivers I have ever had to deal with. We still keep in touch to this day.

Unfortunately, the championship fell apart because there was a petrol crisis in South East Asia and it affected the event in Indonesia, which was cancelled through a lack of petrol. The rallies in Thailand, Malaya and the Philippines were the sort of events where memories are made.

I spent considerable time with Ronan Morgan in 1982. He had co-driven for Tony Pond on several rallies the previous year in a Vauxhall Chevette and was recommended to me by the Blydenstein organization. It was vital that I should benefit from some tarmac testing before the Circuit of Ireland that year, so Ronan and myself tackled the West Cork Rally.

This was my introduction to him, and his local Irish knowledge certainly came to the fore. Ronan insisted that Blydenstein should pay the expenses for several of his friends to travel down from Dublin for the start of the

rally to be observers at stage start lines. He thought it quite likely that various competitors would try and sneak 'fliers', particularly as cars commenced stages at thirty-second intervals. This did happen on at least two occasions in the first seven stages. Billy Coleman, co-driven by Brendan Neville, had a start time one minute behind us and actually started the stages thirty seconds behind us. Ronan's idea of having the observers present was very useful, and by the time Coleman had rolled out of the rally we had posted two enquiries to the event organizers. This highlights some of the problems you can meet when you compete against well known local drivers.

I was very impressed with Ronan's ability to read pace notes. His timing was very good and we had the opportunity to tackle further European events together, with the Blydenstein Chevette, Mike Broad being unable to join me in Europe because of work commitments.

We tackled the Haspengouw Rally in Belgium, where we finished second to the local driver Guy Colsoul in an Ascona 400 – one of the special stages finished outside the bakery the Belgian owned. Ronan made a timing error on the Hunsrück Rally, which cost us two minutes and put us out of contention for the lead.

It was on that event that I very nearly had a huge accident. Many of the stages take place on the Baumholder, an American tank testing ground, and the roads are lined with enormous rocks and stones, called hinkelsteins, to stop tanks sliding off into the undergrowth. On one narrow track through the trees I had a pace note completely wrong and read a medium right-hander as an easy right-hand corner. We bowled into the corner at about 70mph – far too fast – and motored round outside the corner, through the undergrowth, but missed the boulders and hinkelsteins completely. This was one of the biggest scares I have ever had in a rally car. It often seems that the bigger frights are the accidents that don't quite happen. Perhaps there is more time to think about them.

The highlight of the year with Ronan was our outing on the 1,000 Lakes Rally in Finland. The Blydenstein organization was very co-operative and helped us to tackle the event, albeit on a shoestring budget. We gained assistance from Castrol Finland, Helsinki Caravans, Bore Shipping Lines, Pace Petroleum and my regular sponsors, Andrews. This was sufficient to enable us to take two service vans. To cut the cost down we borrowed a car from GM Finland and recce'd the route cheaply, using a caravan for our overnight accommodation. Ronan became tired of my cooking during those two weeks, as we lived on a diet of either porridge or cereal.

The rally itself is relatively cheap to contest once the transportation costs have been overcome. There are few corners in the special stages and consequently you spend a fair proportion of time in fourth and fifth gears, so tyre wear is very low. At the time the route was fairly short compared to other rallies and the roads weren't car damaging. Although many people know the 1,000 Lakes Rally as the event with the jumps, those occur on only four or five stages.

During the recce period we discovered what a difficult job it is for a foreign team to be competitive against the Finns first time out. We managed to recce the first night stage seven times, albeit at a very limited speed because of restrictions, we practised the tests on the third day and second night five times and the others three times. This was our assessment of their importance, but I realized how inadequate this was when I discovered that Ari Vatanen had practised one frequently-used stage 42 times over the years!

Our job was made even more difficult when one of the service vans blew an engine. The mechanics managed to return to Jyvaskala and recover the recce car which was pressed into service. We went on to finish sixth overall, the joint highest finishing position for a non-Scandinavian at the time. I take my hat off to Didier Auriol after his superb third overall in 1988 and more recently Carlos Sainz's incredible win in 1990. It shows how the centre of rallying is moving to Southern Europe.

The other rally I contested with Ronan was the Rally du Vin in Switzerland, which turned out to be a disaster. We battled with Sepp Haider in an Ascona for half the event and managed to lead the rally by five seconds for a time. I then made the big mistake of failing to look out for radar traps and was excluded from the rally for bowling through a small village thirty kph over the official speed limit. We later learned that Swiss drivers lose their driving licences for similar offences.

The half-way halt was at a ski resort called Thynon 2000. There was a long special stage up a mountain to the resort. The service vans set off very early next morning and the road was closed and used as a stage again. All my co-drivers complained that I tended to disappear to the toilet before the start of a rally, but Ronan wasn't aware of this fact and began to panic when our start time neared. He started to look around the hotel for me, while I had returned to the car and was waiting for Ronan Morgan! By the time our start time arrived there was no sign of my co-driver, so one of the mechanics, clad in a rally jacket,

Neil Wilson's knowledge of the British forests has proved particularly useful to Russell in recent rallies. The pair are pictured on the 1990 Cartel International Rally.

Neil Wilson (left) and Russell present a picture of their Texaco Ford Cosworth 4x4 to Miles Walker, the Chief Minister of the Isle of Man, before the start of the 1990 Manx Rally.

sat in the passenger seat over the start ramp and down to the first special stage! This was one of the most exciting rides that Alan Wright ever had.

In 1987 I had the opportunity to tackle the Paris–Dakar Rally, where I met another co-driver whose talents surprised me. At that time service vehicles were not allowed. The only way to support the cars was for factory teams to enter their service trucks in the event. The Opel team and the new Astra 4S, on its only official outing, had a back-up team of three MAN trucks, two 6x6s and one 4x4. I was chosen to drive one of the 350bhp 6x6s, with seven tons of spares on board. Although there were 'flying mechanics' who arrived by air at the bivouacs at night, it was essential that the trucks kept up with the rally time schedule. Not only could they be disqualified if they too were late, but the later the trucks arrived at the overnight halt, the less time the 'flying mechanics' had to work on the rally cars. The event was difficult for Opel, because the cars, being so new, not unexpectedly broke down fairly continually. In the prologue we had not been as fast as the other two vehicles but they lost an enormous amount of time servicing the rally cars. They had an earlier start time than us and kept arriving at the broken-down rally cars before we did. At one point we were lying about 40th overall, in a truck weighing over twenty tons gross. Tony Fall, then Opel Competitions Manager, was desperate that we should remain in the rally, because the other two trucks had incurred in the region of 75 hours of penalties.

We were a crew of three: myself and an Opel mechanic called Ronnie Gardsfeldt, while the third member of the crew was meant to be a navigator and an employee of MAN. He cried off at the last minute and Andy Schultz, a Bavarian freelance mechanic who works for Opel,

stepped in. To my knowledge he had never done any co-driving before. We became lost on the very first special stage along with a large number of other competitors, and we were rescued by one of the organizers' aircraft flying overhead, pointing us in the correct direction by waggling its wings. We were navigating with a compass as well as road books, but Andy Schultz then never made another mistake throughout the whole Paris–Dakar Rally. That was an amazing achievement, and I would recommend him to anybody interested in contesting that event. He is an ideal mechanic and navigator!

I teamed up with Peter Diekmann on the 1988 Circuit of Ireland Rally. I was very impressed with him from the outset, bearing in mind that he had only contested the event once before and I was a driver he had never previously accompanied. His accuracy and skill in delivering pace notes was exemplary, even if quick became 'qvick' in his Germanic accent! Peter is another co-driver who is very aggressive and this is an attribute that I prefer to one of passivity – at least you know that the co-driver is putting everything into his job. Team managers don't seem happy with this attitude and take exception to the demands it places on them and I know that Peter's career has suffered because of this. Some people seem to forget that this is a competitive sport and winning is all important.

The most important job of a co-driver is to get you round a specific route on time and unless someone has the ability to do that then you are on to a loser. You need somebody who has great attention to detail and doesn't overlook little twists and loopholes in the regulations.

A co-driver should ideally also have the ability to organize service plans and service crews, although in

95

PACE NOTE SYSTEM devised by Russell and Peter Bryant

SYMBOL	SPOKEN	EXPLANATION	EXAMPLE
R	Right	Very slight corner	
L	Left		
R̊ L̊	Flat right, left	Flat when dry	
R̊? L̊?	Flat maybe		
Q	Quick	Approx 30 degrees, apex	
E	Easy	Approx 30 degrees, curve	
K	Kay	Approx 60 degrees, apex	
M	Medium	Approx 60 degrees, curve	
B	Bad	Approx 90 degrees, apex	
S	Slow	Approx 90 degrees, curve	
HP	Hairpin	With apex	
OHP	Open hairpin	Curved	
C	Crest	Car does not jump	Flat right over crest R̊/C
J	Jump	Car jumps so indicate speed	SJ
>	Tightens		
<	Opens		
Lg	Long	Cannot be applied to Q, K, B, HP	
VLg	Very long		
SLOWING	Slowing	Shows brake point	
TURN	Turn	Corner or junction	TURN BL
BUMP	Bump	Opposite of jump	

larger teams there is usually a service co-ordinator to handle this requirement. Neil Wilson has been accused by the mechanics of being a lazy co-driver, in that he doesn't like getting too deeply involved in service plans and wants 'everything on a plate'. As he says, those are roles that other people can undertake. He prefers to arrive at an event and work on what is to his mind the essential part of the job which is making sure the driver goes quickly, feels right and is happy with the way he reads pace notes.

Even in Britain reading pace notes is now a fundamental part of the co-driver's repertoire. On events which only allow limited time for practice there is also the need to write them quickly and efficiently. As, I suspect, with most British competitors, my pace notes have grown up on an ad hoc basis, without any formal pattern or reasoning behind them. In the past, pace notes were an exception rather than the norm in Britain, and there were very few techniques to copy. I developed a system evolved out of road rallying and the sort of colloquial descriptions used by a navigator to read roads to you. These were effectively a jumble of terminology used to describe the shape of corners. It was at the end of 1979 that I began to realize the limitations of the system. It was not coherently thought out and didn't enable me to drive much quicker than I would have been able to with eyesight alone. Along with Peter Bryant, I worked out an alternative system

SYMBOL	SPOKEN	EXPLANATION	EXAMPLE
→	Into	Fast corner followed by slow corner	ER → BL
+	And	Two corners almost same speed	MR + ML
	(unspoken pause)	Short distance between corners	MR ML
•	Straight	Distance less than 50 metres	MR • ML
50	Fifty	50 metres	
100	One hundred	100 metres	
200	Two hundred	200 metres	
300	Three hundred	300 metres	
		(Note: never 150 or 250)	

Other words that may sometimes be used:

TIGHT CUT NARROWS WIDENS ROCK KEEP IN STAY OUT

'Medium' can be spoken as 'mid' -- it depends on your accent

The symbols describe the shape of the corner not the speed:

E, M, S, OHP   You drive round so:-

Q, K, B, HP   You clip apex so:-

which was easier to use and enabled me to drive quicker.

It is important to establish very clearly the ground rules of pace notes. This applies to any system, whether it uses numbers or descriptions. There have been many arguments about which is best. If I were starting out in rallying again I would choose the number system because of its greater flexibility and the fact that it enables you to swap from one co-driver to another without undue problems. The English language is well endowed with monosyllabic numbers up to ten (with the exception of seven) which can be spoken quickly.

Many people use a system with number one for the fastest corner. I have never liked this because the pace notes may have been made for a slow car. Later in your career, in a faster car, you may well find that another description is required for a particular corner which was once described as 'flat out'. The number system can cater for that perfectly well: if, for example, seven is a flat corner in a slow car it is then possible to add in the number eight for use with a more powerful rally car.

I was accustomed to a descriptive system, however, and to change would have been dangerously confusing, so Peter Bryant and myself pooled our knowledge and harked back to a technique used by Bernard Darniche in the year that he so convincingly won the European Rally Championship. We decided upon a principle which gave a clear indication of the shape of a corner. I feel that this determines how you drive at a particular corner. A short corner has a different driving style from a very long corner, for example. On a short one you clip the apex of the corner and use the full width of the road on the entrance and exit, while on a long corner you drive round more in the middle of the road.

It is also essential that the terminology can be spoken quickly and the distances are accurate. That may sound obvious, but my experience of seeing other people's notes leads me to the conclusion that most people use inaccurate distances and the grading of corners does vary enormously. Frequently you see notes with unnecessarily small distances on them, such as 10, 20 and 30 metres. If people took the trouble to measure these distances they would realize that 10 metres is so negligible at any speed that it has no consequence in rallying terms. We therefore decided to pick 50 metres as the base distance. Any stretch that was less, but still appeared as a short straight, was simply called 'straight'. We then went up in graduations of 100, avoiding 150 in case I only heard the second half of the instruction and took it to mean 50 metres.

We then divided the corners into two basic shapes; those that you apex and those that are round. Then we found descriptions which would be simple, easy to speak and offered a realistic description of the corner in question. When I drove the Blydenstein car in the same team as Terry Kaby, I could never understand why what to me was a 90-degree right-angle corner to be taken at 25 to 30mph was written as a 'fast K-right' in Terry's notes. 'Fast' hardly seemed the appropriate term.

Using our new system, the grades for rounded corners became 'open hairpin' (it may be a long expression but the corner takes a time to negotiate so the co-driver has time), 'slow' (a rounded corner through 90 degrees), 'mid' (rounded through 60), 'easy' (rounded through 30) and above that, 'flat'. On the corners that you apexed we introduced 'hairpin', 'bad', 'K', 'quick' and 'flat'. We could describe variations by using the words 'opens' and 'tightens' to indicate those bends which may have been sharper or quicker than the basic descriptions suggested. It has turned out to be a very simple system, the notes are easy to make fairly accurately and convey to the driver an instant graphic impression of the shape of a particular corner.

The art of reading pace notes is for a co-driver to get his timing absolutely correct. If he reads the notes too late, the driver becomes unsure of the forthcoming corner and the instinctive reaction is to brake. On the other hand, if he reads the note too early it is easy to forget about the instruction. In the end, it doesn't matter too much what the actual descriptions are, provided that the co-driver sorts out his timing.

Unless a co-driver is particularly experienced, you must be very careful to ensure that the phrases are written accurately. They should not be in a continuous, unbroken sequence: I feel that each line of pace notes should be phrased to end with either a definite distance or a very

slow corner to provide a natural break point in the co-driver's reading.

Many roads have telegraph poles along their length, but few people realize that the poles are either 30 or 50 metres apart. By counting the number of poles it is easy to build up a picture of the distances along special stages.

For the first two or three years of the pace note system I used the word 'absolute' to denote a corner which was of no consequence, implying 'absolutely flat'. West Baldwin, a stage on the Isle of Man, cured me of using that word ever again. When I contested the Manx Rally in a Chevette with Mike Broad, it became apparent that it was a term which took too long to speak properly. We ultimately replaced it with just either 'right' or 'left', which also means that I had the flexibility of being able to add them to other instructions, for example 'right, turn bad left' to indicate that the road kicked right just before the main corner.

There is a great temptation to believe that pace notes even out competition for everybody, but it is worthwhile remembering that this is certainly not the case. Should you have the opportunity (and mental capacity!) to memorize a road instead, then that is the best thing to do. A classic illustration is the fact that the 1,000 Lakes Rally has rarely been won by a Swedish driver and the Swedish Rally has rarely been won by a Finn. If pace notes made everything equal, then one could expect the wins to have been equally split. In fact, of course, it is much easier for a Finnish driver to practise the roads on the 1,000 Lakes and learn them intimately and a Swede those in Sweden simply because of geography and local familiarity. The performance advantage to be gained by driving from memory compared with using pace notes is greater than the improvement pace notes provide over driving on sight alone.

Secret route rallies are obviously very different from pace note events, and I find the most important asset there is a co-driver who will only read factually correct information. There is a great temptation to generalize from the map and this is very detrimental to a fast performance, because it introduces an element of doubt into a driver's mind. If the co-driver can't pass on really accurate and useful information he should shut up!

Co-drivers are a peculiar breed of people: they take the same risks as a driver without having any direct control over the situation, so they can end up having someone else's accident! They don't usually attract any of the attention the driver gets at the end of an event, either.

In some ways, co-drivers are like ladies' handbags, because they are useful for taking along all the little odds and ends like whistles, screwdrivers, penknives, anti-midge cream, eye drops, sweets – the list is endless. Martin Holmes used to take a little box of goodies which he called 'The Compleat Navigator'. Like them or loathe them, you can't do without co-drivers – though maybe one day we shall have a satellite navigation robot in the second seat!

7

Successful sponsorship

The most common question at any rally forum is 'How do I get sponsorship?' The prospect of having someone else pay even part of the ever-increasing cost of your rallying is obviously an enticing one, and you might think, judging from the multitude of company names and brand logos to be seen at any reasonably large motorsport meeting, that there was plenty of money about. But the plain fact is that, if you haven't a good track record in the sport already, it is very difficult to attract support unless you are very lucky – or a bit of a con artist! Among the key things possible sponsors will want to know is that the team they invest in has a reasonable chance of success and will be handled professionally. So unless the driver can prove that he has been competing successfully, finding sponsorship is an uphill struggle.

One of the first things to do is to research the company you are approaching. Who would actually be responsible for signing off the sponsorship? Which department or person handles the request? Would the company want to promote a group of products? Are there separate product divisions with different managers who need to become involved? If it is a small company, does the Managing Director or some other important individual have an interest in motorsport? What are company finances like? You should visit one of the company locations to see how the company promotes itself and get a feel for what type of company it is.

It is vital that you turn everything on its head and look at the situation from the potential sponsor's point of view. The all-too-usual approach for sponsorship can be boiled down to 'Me and me mate are goin' rallying: give us £1,000 and we'll paint yer name on the side of the car!' If you think I'm over-simplifying, Mike Gilligan, of County Garages, Carlisle, once received almost exactly such a letter from two would-be works drivers. It's not hard to see that such a proposition is of limited appeal, to put it mildly.

Remember that there is no shortage of other forms of publicity, all loudly claiming that they can deliver the goods to the advertiser. Anyone considering sponsorship is going to be asking whether the money is being well spent and whether the investment will bring a worthwhile return. If you start to answer those questions, you begin to formulate your own approach to prospective sponsors.

You have to try to demonstrate that by sponsoring your car the sponsor will actually increase his sales of a particular product or service and generate enough profit to pay for the agreement. This is difficult to quantify, but an attempt to do it shows that you have made the effort to understand the sponsor's position. Alternatively, the general publicity value can be estimated and expressed in terms of how much it would cost at a commercial rate in some other advertising medium. For many years Andrews requested that their salesmen ticked a little box on an order form if they felt that the rally sponsorship had influenced that particular sale.

If the decision is to come from one individual, it is worth including personal perks which make it worthwhile for them; something along the lines of their being able to get involved with the team and be part of the sport as an insider, which is always more attractive than being just a spectator. It is of course acceptable to involve sponsors in your sport like this – straight cash payments are not!

Very few sponsors have the facility – or the inclination – to put large sums of money up front, and as far as possible the deal should be arranged so that the sponsor becomes involved on a stage payment basis. The classic example was my first agreement with Andrews Industrial Equipment in 1974. They were new to the sport, unsure how the idea would work out, and John Andrews suggested an arrangement which let him in gently. There was an initial payment of £1,000 and I was then paid £20 for every event start, £20 for every finish and £20 for

The 1974 Donegal Rally was Russell's first event with Andrews Heat for Hire support.

every class win. At the end of the season the sum was made up to £1,500 if I won either of the two championships I was contesting.

This arrangement got the rally programme off the ground and gave the sponsor the comfort of knowing that he was only paying when the car appeared on a rally and when it won. It is an approach I would always recommend because it is useful in convincing a sponsor that the money is being spent wisely by allowing them to monitor the progress of the venture. It is also conducive to a long-term relationship which is of much more value than a one-off shot however generous.

In addition to outlining your basic proposal and explaining your ambitions in the sport, you then have to demonstrate to a potential sponsor that you have the capability to utilize the money successfully and give as much as possible in return. The obvious factor is publicity, and a major task is to get to know your local sports reporter and the journalists at *Motoring News* and *Autosport*. If these people know you, there is more chance

that something about your rallying activities will appear in their columns.

Probably the most important contacts early on will be at local level. You will find that most local newspapers have very small editorial staffs with little time to put copy together. They will be grateful to receive accurate information and you will more often than not find your copy appearing word for word in the paper if it has been well edited beforehand. Newspapers will shy away from going overboard with mentions for sponsors but a good photograph does an excellent job and is a sure way of obtaining some publicity. It is well worth finding out by name the people to whom press releases should be sent.

Make contact with your local radio station, get to know the people there and show your sponsor that they take an interest in your activities. It may well be worth carrying the name of a local newspaper or television station on the car. It can be double-edged but it is certainly a useful route to obtaining publicity. In my early career the Escort carried the name of the *Birmingham Post* and this

The *Birmingham Post* newspaper helped to support Russell and John Brown in this Escort RS2000.

guaranteed good coverage in that paper. The double edge was that no other newspaper mentioned us at all, as they would have been promoting the opposition. Don't expect the local radio station or newspaper to put money into the project, just treat it as a way of getting publicity. They will feel that their contribution is the coverage that they give you during the year.

This is an excellent way of demonstrating to a sponsor that you are ensuring plenty of exposure. The first time I used this approach was in the early days with John Brown. We had won the first quarterly award in the Mexico Championship, which was two works drives on national rallies, but we persuaded Stuart Turner that one of these outings should be the RAC Rally. We did this by going to ATV, the Midlands television company, and asking them to sponsor the car. Their immediate response was negative, no money was available, but John explained that we didn't want money.

What we asked them to do was to promote our car throughout the rally by television coverage. John convinced them that we would be an exciting team to follow, particularly as the event passed through a number of stages in the Midlands. We also made arrangements, through other contacts in motorsport, for ATV to be fed with additional footage throughout the rally at a very

moderate cost. With ATV on board, we approached Dunlop and persuaded them to supply tyres with the incentive of having a television station behind us. We then went to Ford with a complete package, and they were prepared to supply the car, service vans and parts for us to tackle the RAC Rally. It was then a relatively simple matter to get other sponsors – Redmond Heenan Froude, the dynamometer manufacturers, and Castrol – to inject the final cash element into the project.

In that way a link with a local television station was the starting point in setting up an RAC Rally programme, even though ATV didn't donate any cash. It would be nice to say that the result was equally successful, but I rolled in Sutton Park – at least it was in front of the television cameras! It provided them with dramatic footage which was used for years afterwards.

A driver should always remain aware that sponsorship is going to have to be paid for out of increased sales, and it may be that the sponsor has a product which is of interest to another company involved in the rally programme. It is always a good idea to introduce the relevant people over a meal, to enable relationships to develop and these commercial opportunities to thrive. There is an excellent chance to foster goodwill through reciprocal commerce.

'Here Comes Russell Brookes' – from the archives, a promotional brochure which Russell used to attract support in 1975.

Here Comes Russell Brookes

"one of the most talented young rally drivers"
Judith Jackson, SUNDAY TIMES, 7 July 1974
"rated by many as the top up and coming driver in Britain today"
BIRMINGHAM POST Avon Motor Tour of Britain Special Supplement, July 1974
"extremely methodical, and extremely dedicated, and extremely professional and extremely fast"
AUTOSPORT, 25 July 1974
"the driver who won more rallies in '73 than any body else"
Richard Hudson-Evans, FAST CAR, July 1974
"the Mexico performances of Brookes . . . are a legend"
AUTOSPORT, 7 February 1974
"the performance expected from Russell is now becoming almost a legend"
AUTOSPORT, 19 September 1974

Forums have long been a part of promotional work. With Russell here are Colin Wilson (RAC MSA Press Officer) and *Top Gear*'s Tony Mason, winning co-driver on the 1972 RAC Rally.

102

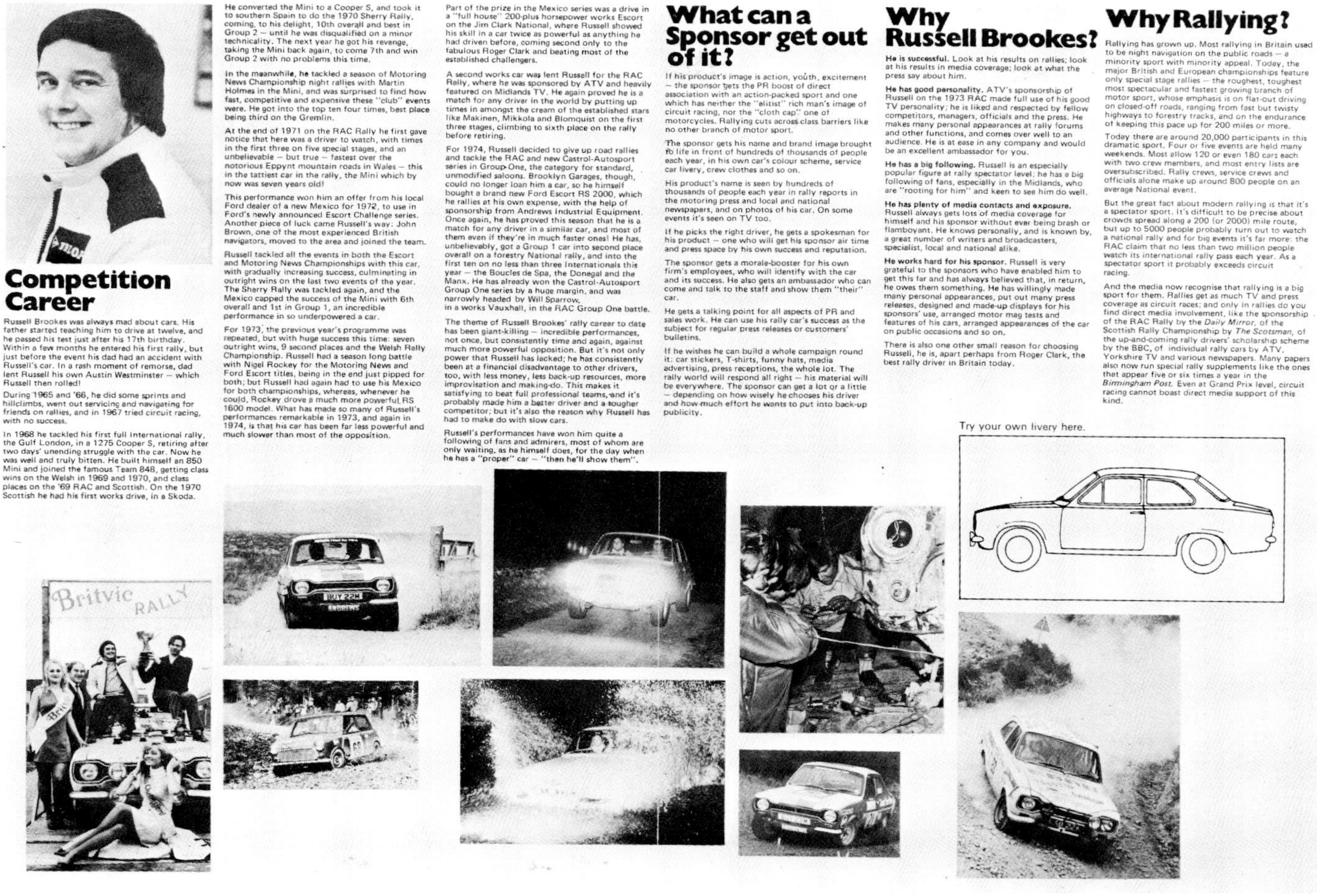

Competition Career

Russell Brookes was always mad about cars. His father started teaching him to drive at twelve, and he passed his test just after his 17th birthday. Within a few months he entered his first rally, but just before the event his dad had an accident with Russell's car. In a rash moment of remorse, dad lent Russell his own Austin Westminster – which Russell then rolled!

During 1965 and '66, he did some sprints and hillclimbs, went out servicing and navigating for friends on rallies, and in 1967 tried circuit racing, with no success.

In 1968 he tackled his first full International rally, the Gulf London, in a 1275 Cooper S, retiring after two days' unending struggle with the car. Now he was well and truly bitten. He built himself an 850 Mini and joined the famous Team 848, getting class wins on the Welsh in 1969 and 1970, and class places on the '69 RAC and Scottish. On the 1970 Scottish he had his first works drive, in a Skoda.

He converted the Mini to a Cooper S, and took it to southern Spain to do the 1970 Sherry Rally, coming, to his delight, 10th overall and best in Group 2 – until he was disqualified on a minor technicality. The next year he got his revenge, taking the Mini back again, to come 7th and win Group 2 with no problems this time.

In the meanwhile, he tackled a season of Motoring News Championship night rallies with Martin Holmes in the Mini, and was surprised to find how fast, competitive and expensive these "club" events were. He got into the top ten four times, best place being third on the Gremlin.

At the end of 1971 on the RAC Rally he first gave notice that here was a driver to watch, with times in the first three on five special stages, and an unbelievable – but true – fastest over the notorious Eppynt mountain roads in Wales – this in the tattiest car in the rally, the Mini which by now was seven years old!

This performance won him an offer from his local Ford dealer of a new Mexico for 1972, to use in Ford's newly announced Escort Challenge series. Another piece of luck came Russell's way: John Brown, one of the most experienced British navigators, moved to the area and joined the team.

Russell tackled all the events in both the Escort and Motoring News Championships with this car, with gradually increasing success, culminating in outright wins on the last two events of the year. The Sherry Rally was tackled again, and the Mexico capped the success of the Mini with 6th overall and 1st in Group 1, an incredible performance in so underpowered a car.

For 1973, the previous year's programme was repeated, but with huge success this time: seven outright wins, 9 second places and the Welsh Rally Championship. Russell had a season long battle with Nigel Rockey for the Motoring News and Ford Escort titles, being in the end just pipped for both; but Russell had again had to use his Mexico for both championships, whereas, whenever he could, Rockey drove a much more powerful RS 1600 model. What has made so many of Russell's performances remarkable in 1973, and again in 1974, is that his car has been far less powerful and much slower than most of the opposition.

Part of the prize in the Mexico series was a drive in a "full house" 200-plus horsepower works Escort on the Jim Clark National, where Russell showed his skill in a car twice as powerful as anything he had driven before, coming second only to the fabulous Roger Clark and beating most of the established challengers.

A second works car was lent Russell for the RAC Rally, where he was sponsored by ATV and heavily featured on Midlands TV. He again proved he is a match for any driver in the world by putting up times in amongst the cream of the established stars like Makinen, Mikkola and Blomquist on the first three stages, climbing to sixth place on the rally before retiring.

For 1974, Russell decided to give up road rallies and tackle the RAC and new Castrol-Autosport series in Group One, the category for standard, unmodified saloons. Brooklyn Garages, though, could no longer loan him a car, so he himself bought a brand new Ford Escort RS 2000, which he rallies at his own expense, with the help of sponsorship from Andrews Industrial Equipment. Once again, he has proved this season that he is a match for any driver in a similar car, and most of them even if they're in much faster ones! He has, unbelievably, got a Group 1 car into second place overall on a forestry National rally, and into the first ten on no less than three Internationals this year – the Boucles de Spa, the Donegal and the Manx. He has already won the Castrol-Autosport Group One series by a huge margin, and was narrowly headed by Will Sparrow, in a works Vauxhall, in the RAC Group One battle.

The theme of Russell Brookes' rally career to date has been giant-killing – incredible performances, not once, but consistently time and again, against much more powerful opposition. But it's not only power that Russell has lacked; he has consistently been at a financial disadvantage to other drivers, too, with less money, less back-up resources, more improvisation and making-do. This makes it satisfying to beat full professional teams, and it's probably made him a better driver and a tougher competitor; but it's also the reason why Russell has had to make do with slow cars.

Russell's performances have won him quite a following of fans and admirers, most of whom are only waiting, as he himself does, for the day when he has a "proper" car – "then he'll show them".

What can a Sponsor get out of it?

If his product's image is action, youth, excitement – the sponsor gets the PR boost of direct association with an action-packed sport and one which has neither the "elitist" rich man's image of circuit racing, nor the "cloth cap" one of motorcycles. Rallying cuts across class barriers like no other branch of motor sport.

The sponsor gets his name and brand image brought to life in front of hundreds of thousands of people each year, in his own car's colour scheme, service car livery, crew clothes and so on.

His product's name is seen by hundreds of thousands of people each year in rally reports in the motoring press and local and national newspapers, and on photos of his car. On some events it's seen on TV too.

If he picks the right driver, he gets a spokesman for his product – one who will get his sponsor air time and press space by his own success and reputation.

The sponsor gets a morale-booster for his own firm's employees, who will identify with the car and its success. He also gets an ambassador who can come and talk to the staff and show them "their" car.

He gets a talking point for all aspects of PR and sales work. He can use his rally car's success as the subject for regular press releases or customers' bulletins.

If he wishes he can build a whole campaign round it: car stickers, T-shirts, funny hats, media advertising, press receptions, the whole lot. The rally world will respond all right – his material will be everywhere. The sponsor can get a lot or a little – depending on how wisely he chooses his driver and how much effort he wants to put into back-up publicity.

Why Russell Brookes?

He is successful. Look at his results on rallies; look at his results in media coverage; look at what the press say about him.

He has good personality. ATV's sponsorship of Russell on the 1973 RAC made full use of his good TV personality; he is liked and respected by fellow competitors, managers, officials and the press. He makes many personal appearances at rally forums and other functions, and comes over well to an audience. He is at ease in any company and would be an excellent ambassador for you.

He has a big following. Russell is an especially popular figure at rally spectator level; he has a big following of fans, especially in the Midlands, who are "rooting for him" and keen to see him do well.

He has plenty of media contacts and exposure. Russell always gets lots of media coverage for himself and his sponsor without ever being brash or flamboyant. He knows personally, and is known by, a great number of writers and broadcasters, specialist, local and national alike.

He works hard for his sponsor. Russell is very grateful to the sponsors who have enabled him to get this far and has always believed that, in return, he owes them something. He has willingly made many personal appearances, put out many press releases, designed and made-up displays for his sponsors' use, arranged motor mag tests and features of his cars, arranged appearances of the car on public occasions and so on.

There is also one other small reason for choosing Russell, he is, apart perhaps from Roger Clark, the best rally driver in Britain today.

Why Rallying?

Rallying has grown up. Most rallying in Britain used to be night navigation on the public roads – a minority sport with minority appeal. Today, the major British and European championships feature only special stage rallies – the roughest, toughest most spectacular and fastest growing branch of motor sport, whose emphasis is on flat-out driving on closed-off roads, ranging from fast but twisty highways to forestry tracks, and on the endurance of keeping this pace up for 200 miles or more.

Today there are around 20,000 participants in this dramatic sport. Four or five events are held many weekends. Most allow 120 or even 180 cars each with two crew members, and most entry lists are oversubscribed. Rally crews, service crews and officials alone make up around 800 people on an average National event.

But the great fact about modern rallying is that it's a spectator sport. It's difficult to be precise about crowds spread along a 200 (or 2000) mile route, but up to 5000 people probably turn out to watch a national rally and for big events it's far more: the RAC claim that no less than two million people watch its international rally pass each year. As a spectator sport it probably exceeds circuit racing.

And the media now recognise that rallying is a big sport for them. Rallies get as much TV and press coverage as circuit races; and only in rallies do you find direct media involvement, like the sponsorship of the RAC Rally by the *Daily Mirror*, of the Scottish Rally Championship by *The Scotsman*, of the up-and-coming rally drivers' scholarship scheme by the BBC, of individual rally cars by ATV, Yorkshire TV and various newspapers. Many papers also now run special rally supplements like the ones that appear five or six times a year in the *Birmingham Post*. Even at Grand Prix level, circuit racing cannot boast direct media support of this kind.

Try your own livery here.

It is essential that you attempt to bring the sport into your sponsor's company. If you are good at talking in front of people, one of the things you can do is to take your rally car along and make a presentation to your sponsor's staff and customers. Arranging a rally evening is good for raising the level of interest within the company, and a manager will find it a good way to entertain his customers, something which company people often find difficult to do effectively. If a sales manager decides to take a potential client and his wife out for a meal, you are talking about a large bill for something which is usually forgotten within a week. You can point out that a rally team provides an opportunity for entertaining customers, perhaps on the premises, with something more interesting than product talk.

Andrews have taken advantage of rally films in this way at their trade evenings. But it is worth remembering that anything longer than 20 minutes becomes boring for an audience not entirely composed of rally fanatics. We used 10-minute comedy films, the favourite being a W C Fields car chase from the 1930s, to break up the evening. Customers will also want to hear about your rally programme first hand, so it is as well to learn how to address a gathering with confidence. Humorous public speaking is an art in itself, though, and unless you have a natural talent I believe it is best to leave the 'one-liners' alone. A good idea is to have postcards and stickers available which can be given to those present for their children.

Another way in which the rally car can be used, one which is not often undertaken, is to take customers for rides in it. I've found this to be one of the most outstanding promotions you can carry out, having done it for Andrews on numerous occasions in the past. We know that people we took out back in 1981 still ring the factory and ask when there is going to be another opportunity to ride in the rally car. Such functions are surprisingly difficult to organize, however, because you need a good venue which is within reach of your sponsor's customers. You should really have two cars available, because you cannot risk spoiling the day with a mechanical breakdown, and it is important to have someone on hand to maintain the organization while you are out in the car. Most importantly, you must have adequate insurance: an accident is always a possibility and it would be a great disaster to have a customer injured and then find that there was no insurance cover. For these reasons, it is better to stick to a

Peter Webber, the Managing Director of Andrews Sykes Limited.

rally show when you're starting out, rather than trying to run such a 'customer special stage day'.

One of the most exciting promotional projects I have been involved in recently was the 'Rally Waltzers Display' at the 1989 Birmingham Super Prix. The idea was borrowed from a similar exercise at the official opening of the new Nürburgring in Germany. That was put together by Tony Fall and Rauno Aaltonen and featured nine works Opel Mantas. With the minimum level of practice, we had to carry out forward spins, reverse spins and handbrake turns, in unison, at various points around the circuit. It went off very well indeed, except for one instance when Erwin Weber, the German rally driver, stalled in front of me. Rather than hold up the proceedings, I got up behind his car, punted him in the rear and enabled him to jump start his engine. This incident caused damage to both cars and I was surprised to discover later that this had started a bitter financial wrangle between Opel Germany and Vauxhall UK. The former claimed that the damage to Weber's car had been caused by my car running into the back of him.

In spite of that, this project so impressed me that I decided to arrange a similar session at Birmingham using the four Andrews Sierra Cosworths that Mark Lovell and I then had at our disposal. I was joined by Mark, Gwyndaf Evans and Stig Blomqvist, and together we put on a tyre-smoking display for the spectators as a sample of what rallying was all about. The only problem from a promotional point of view was that we generated so much tyre smoke that most of the onlookers said they couldn't see the cars!

The slowest promotional outings that the Andrews Sykes rally cars have been involved in were pace-car duties at a number of top cycle races where it was necessary to average 25mph and keep just ahead of the

Andrews used the rally cars many times to add interest to charity events. This is the Manta 400 at a sports day for the disabled.

Russell's 1980 rally car and service barge outside the Andrews headquarters in Wolverhampton.

leaders. Every time, we remembered to put in a set of soft spark plugs and replace them before the car was used for competition again.

Certainly, the Andrews years have been hard work, and there was a period when the rally car and myself were in enormous demand for trade and publicity evenings. The busiest year was 1978, after my first British Open Championship title, when I appeared at 54 promotional functions at venues as far apart as Aberdeen and Plymouth. This was in addition to the rally forums organized by Ford, and all the other rally activities.

I have been fortunate to have retained the Andrews sponsorship for a long time. Partly, that is a matter of

luck, partly it is because of the nature of their products, and a third reason has been this continued hard work.

The element of luck for me was the timing of the approach back in 1974. Andrews was a relatively small company at that time, with a turnover of around £850,000. This almost doubled annually for five or six years after the sponsorship began and this rapid growth meant that Andrews' ability to support my rallying grew in step with the progression of my career, starting at the time when I moved from being an amateur driver in a Group 1 RS2000 to a full works car and a works contract. It would have been easy for my progress to outstrip the available support, or for their requirements to reach

Russell took part in the 1986 British Truck Grand Prix, finishing second in the up-to-300bhp class final in this Renault, in Andrews colours of course.

105

STW 180R sits proudly outside the Andrews premises. This car was a replica RS1800, and had been the prototype for the Escort 1300 Championship specification. In that form, it took a top-ten finish on the Tour of Epynt with John Horton co-driving.

Andrews Heat for Hire expanded their motorsport sponsorship beyond rallying for a time and gave support to Ross Hockenhull's racing programme.

Andrews always made good use of the rallying programme to gain media exposure, and pushed the message home with leaflets, posters and display material.

Many a rally marshal has longed for Heat for Hire! Andrews christmas card picks up the winter rally theme.

Rallying offered Andrews an ideal way of marketing their products, as this photograph demonstrates. Russell shows off the silverware – with just a little historical licence in the simultaneous appearance of the Chevette, Talbot Sunbeam and Escort!

Russell proudly displays the Andrews Chevette outside his new printing premises in Redditch – the town's Development Corporation appreciated the publicity value, too.

The 'Rally Waltzers' display was put on in conjunction with the Birmingham Super Prix in 1989 and featured four Sierra RS Cosworth rally cars.

From left to right, Russell, Gwyndaf Evans, Mark Lovell and Stig Blomqvist discuss plans for the 'Rally Waltzers'.

beyond a rally team which had stayed static, but we were able to develop together. Of course, the increased turnover was solely because of the publicity value of rallying, according to me!

The type of products Andrews sell turned out to be another important factor. The company hires out portable heaters as well as selling water heaters, air conditioning, industrial and agricultural pumps, building drying equipment and office cleaning gear. The people specifically involved in this type of equipment were often the very people who were interested in rallying. Time and again when we toured companies in an effort to generate business for Andrews Sykes, we found that we were talking to people enthusiastic about motorsport – not generally the managing directors, but the works engineers and sales managers, and it is they who sign the orders.

If you were trying to sell something to the managing directors of large public companies, you might very well find that, with a few exceptions, rallying was not their sport. They would be more interested in yacht racing or going to Ascot and having champagne in the hospitality tent.

Hard work was the third element which made the sponsorship arrangement so successful. As a company, Andrews have always believed in doing things themselves – it comes from the personal beliefs of the directors. They have always pushed people to make use of the team and a lot of publicity has revolved around the rallying programme. I was always encouraged to meet many companies and visit other factories and talk to potential customers. This paid off because we always seemed to make a substantial breakthrough in terms of additional sales where the opening introductions had been through an interest in the rally team.

Examples of this included the contacts made by Andrews in the Talbot factories when I drove for Des O'Dell and the Talbot team. Until that time the Coventry factories had been a closed shop as far as the Andrews group of companies was concerned, but it seemed that the rallying association opened doors that were closed to the more conventional sales approaches.

When we moved to GM, Andrews' sales people were hitting their heads against a brick wall when it came to selling heating and air conditioning equipment into the Vauxhall factories at Luton and Bedford. Two years into the sponsorship, I decided to have a go at cracking the problem myself. I was visiting the Luton plant near where the rally Astra project was based, and decided to ask a man on the production line what he did if he felt cold. He pointed me in the direction of the foreman, who directed me to the works engineer, who told me the name of the buyer through whom he placed an order. I went along to visit the buyer and out of that came an introduction for the Andrews sales force. Two months later they received an order for over £100,000 worth of heating equipment to be used in the factory.

It is that sort of hard work and persistence from everybody in the company which makes a sponsorship deal so successful, to the mutual benefit of both parties. Unless a good deal of effort is put into generating publicity, nothing will come out of a sponsorship programme and that ultimately works to the detriment of both driver and team. There have been many examples where sponsors put money into a project and then sit back and do nothing, before reflecting at the end of the year on the money which has been wasted: that was never the case at Andrews Sykes. One of the hardest things for a rally team can be making sure that a sponsor gets value for money by pushing them along to exploit the possibilities. I have been fortunate in that Andrews as a company and John Andrews in person have always been willing to become involved in my programme in order to reap the benefits of my success.

8

Giving it a go

Giving it a go is something which a considerable number of rally drivers fail to do. Rallying is a competitive sport and the most important thing of all is to drive as fast as possible. Sounds obvious – yet one of the most amazing misconceptions held by rally drivers, one I have seen evidence of on numerous occasions and one which has been promoted by people who purport to be experts in this field, is that it is possible to take it easy during the first half of a rally, play yourself in over a few early stages, see how everybody else is fairing, and then, later on, drive faster and catch up. This ignores one of the fundamentals of life: time lost can never be regained.

Once a second has been lost it is impossible to regain that time, and that rule should govern your attitude to driving. The idea that you can start to speed up and recover that time is an absolute fallacy and merely indicates you should have been driving faster in the first place. The best analogy is with golf: a Faldo or a Woosnam never says, 'I'll cruise through the first round and maybe drop ten shots to the leaders and see how they are doing and then I'll catch up in the next round.' This is just not possible and nor is it for a rally driver. When golfers step up to their ball they don't consider the shots that have gone before, nor do they think of the shots that are coming in the future, except possibly the one immediately afterwards, but they concentrate on playing the stroke to the best of their ability every time. Once they have played that shot they try to forget it and go on to the next one.

This is very similar to rallying because, when you start a special stage, really all you should be considering is driving the next corner as best as you possibly can without damaging the car, and putting yourself in a position where you can progress to take the following corner as fast as possible.

Having negotiated that corner, you have mentally to set aside anything untoward that happened, be it a spin or a mechanical problem or just that you went too slowly, and concentrate on doing the next corner as well as possible. When you have completed 150 corners as well as possible you then have a fast stage time, and when you've completed 50 stages you have an RAC Rally. The problem with many people is that they think of an event in its entirety, rather than setting out to attack to the maximum of their ability from the outset.

This doesn't mean to say that you will drive the first special stage as well as the fifth or the tenth, because you will have played yourself in and will naturally be faster as you get into the rally. What is important is that you don't hold anything back and that you try to drive every corner of every stage as quickly as possible within the prevailing circumstances.

If you accept the necessity to drive every corner to the best of your ability with regard to the conditions and preserving the car, it then follows that you must be mentally and physically prepared to give your best at the start of each stage. On so many occasions I have seen people arrive at stage starts in a big panic, mentally flustered and probably still fastening the belts, when they should be calm and collected and ready to focus all their attention and ability.

It is always important, and in many ways this is the co-driver's role, to ensure that there is a brief period before the start of a test where you can compose yourself. Walter Röhrl seemed to have a ritual he would meticulously go through before stage starts to gain his composure and concentration. I noticed more than once that he'd take time to pull on his driving gloves gently and smooth them out quite slowly and deliberately over each finger. The process took about a minute to complete and was clearly designed to take his mind away from other troubles. Something of this nature could well be adopted by any driver.

Keeping up with competitive pressure through darkness and difficult conditions is what brings success in rallying. The Manta crashes through the icy waters of a Yorkshire stream during the 1987 National Breakdown Rally.

To maximize your performance it is very important that the car is set up properly in advance, for having to fiddle with the brake balance bar on a stage, for example, can ruin your concentration. There seems to be a general consensus among clubman that, if your car is equipped with a brake bias adjustment, it should be set so that the rear wheels lock first and force the tail of the vehicle to slide out easily.

This is absolutely incorrect. The ideal method is that, whatever the surface, all four wheels should lock up together. If this is not possible to achieve it is better to have the bias set slightly to the front wheels so that they lock fractionally sooner than the rears. Where the misconception comes from is that if the surface is very slippery, it is necessary to move the bias gradually from the front to the rear wheels. The less grip, the less is the weight transfer that takes place from the rear to the front

of the car under braking, and this reduces the braking effort which can be transmitted through the front wheels. Regardless of whether you are driving on tarmac, on forest gravel or on ice, however, the ideal setting is where all four wheels lock up together or something very close to that.

One of the big problems with having the bias set heavily to the rear occurs when you have a panic situation on the approach to a corner, hit the brakes too hard and lock the wheels. In a similar way to a handbrake turn, this often results in a spin and the car goes off the road backwards. If the front wheels lock fractionally before the rears you achieve the maximum braking effort and there is a weight transfer which forces the front of the car to dig in and pull the nose in towards the corner. It is then possible to ease off slightly and the car can be pulled very tightly into a corner with maximum braking efficiency whilst it remains stable.

112

A service plan should be arranged well in advance to minimize the risk of delays. Russell's Escort is attended to during the New Zealand Rally in 1977.

In a four-wheel-drive vehicle, where all four wheels are connected together, it is difficult to measure how the brakes have been set up, and it is common policy to have a mechanic stand at the end of a special stage to measure the temperature of the brake discs. He can then tell whether each disc has contributed a similar level of braking effort. Even with four-wheel-drive the brake bias is important because the centre differential will usually allow at least the first stab on the brakes to act more on the front or rear and influence the car's behaviour accordingly. Some of the more sophisticated systems incorporate a means of decoupling the front and rear to allow the use of the handbrake.

It is these problems with brake bias which are often the cause of the very untidy and sideways driving techniques we see in club rallying. It is important to keep the speed up in any type of car, but on loose surfaces many people drive far too sideways. The net effect is that they scrub off speed, and disregard the important rule of driving around corners as smoothly as possible. From my own

observations, the quick times have always been recorded when the car has been driven as near as possible to the perfect racing line, be it in the forests or on tarmac.

Another important area is to ensure the optimum level of grip at the front to improve the ability of the car to turn into a corner. It is noticeable that the more a vehicle understeers (a tendency to slide straight on at corners), the more the driver has to compensate by setting it up sideways into a corner, losing speed in the process. If the machine has been set up with good front-end grip this is less necessary. It is therefore vital to spend time sorting out front suspension spring and damper rates, finding the correct level of negative camber (important in terms of the car's ability to turn in) and adjusting the geometry to provide the optimum level of castor.

On most cars increasing the castor angle generates negative camber on the front suspension as the steering is turned and this helps the outside front tyre bite and turn the nose into the corner. Running a few minutes extra toe-in on the front wheel alignment can sometimes help, but care should always be taken to ensure that the straight-line stability of the car does not suffer.

Once you have started a special stage one of the greatest qualities which comes to light is the ability to anticipate circumstances. This boils down to eyesight and it is important that a driver looks a long way ahead when driving a rally car. There is a great tendency to look too closely at the road immediately ahead. If you have confidence in your own abilities, there will be time to look around and study the road ahead. Specifically on secret route events you may drive down a forest road and see the track emerging from a valley the other side. It is therefore possible to assume that you are approaching a corner and you are able to guess where it may be. Where logging operations have taken place, roads can often be covered in mud. It's amazing how many people don't read the situation in advance and begin to brake on the muddy patches where they cannot control the car, instead of slowing before the mud and crossing it with power on, all cars being most stable under gentle acceleration.

Similarly, if you can see a large puddle it is best to prepare yourself by switching on the wipers before the water and being aware that the car may be dragged to one side slightly if you touch the puddle with one wheel. It may even be quicker to drive around the water.

This question of anticipation leads on to another factor, to which club-level drivers rarely pay enough attention, and that is the obvious one of ensuring that the windscreen is spotlessly clean at all times. If there are specks of dirt and squashed flies on the screen it is amazing how your eyesight shuts down and you end up looking at the marks on the glass rather than the road far ahead. I have always insisted that the windscreen on my rally car is changed during the year to ensure that it is free of gravel pit marks and the accumulation of tiny scratches which gradually reduce its transparency.

Competing in daylight is obviously the easiest form of rallying but even here distracting reflections can occur in bright sunshine, particularly off the back of spotlights when they are still fitted. It is a good idea to paint the backs of these items matt black or to take then off in daylight – lamps are expensive to replace in the case of an accident, too, which is another good reason.

Some windscreen wiper blades can be dazzling, but the biggest single problem is the glare and reflections which emanate from the top of the dashboard and switches and controls within the car. It is now possible to obtain a non-reflective fabric material which can be placed over the top of the console to stop the reflections. This has been a great aid for me. It is also necessary to check the cowling around the co-driver's equipment, for very often the LED crystal display from the tripmeter will reflect on the screen.

On the RAC Rally you are often prone to one of the most dangerous conditions, when the sun is very low in the sky even in the daytime so you can come over a crest and find it shining directly into your eyes. Visors don't work in these situations and I recommend the use of a long peak on your helmet: it is then an easy matter to tilt

your head forwards to cut out the glare. This is another situation which highlights the importance of having a clean windscreen.

A classic example of a driver being blinded by the sun was Hannu Mikkola's accident whilst leading the 1988 RAC Rally in a Mazda. This was all the more surprising, as Hannu was the first driver I knew who used a long peak on his helmet and it was through him that I learned the technique. If ever there was a case of relearning old lessons . . .

One of the recent innovations that I don't like is the heated windscreen. I find the reflections off the heating wires very distracting and this is something that I don't want in my rally cars. I prefer to ensure that the heating and demisting systems are working correctly and can cope with any situation that may arise – though sometimes things go wrong.

On the 1990 Cartel International Rally I was out for the first time in the new Sierra 2.9i 4x4. The fresh-air intake pipe was just underneath the wheelarch and it was collecting a fair amount of water which was then vaporized by the heater and blown on to the windscreen. This turned out to be a major problem and the R-E-D mechanics spent a lot of time trying to relocate the pipe and attempting to find some demister fluid to smear on the screen. If there are no garages around a good substitute for demister fluid is a sliced potato rubbed on to the screen!

Driving at dusk poses another problem. When the sun is fading, drivers often put their headlamps and spotlights on far too early. No matter how good the lighting, you can never see as clearly all round as you can without them. One of the things which happens is that you get pools of light shining in the road immediately ahead of the car and your eyesight closes down to that point. It is usually possible to drive quicker by leaving the lights switched off until quite late when the conditions are almost dark.

For rallying in darkness the importance of good lighting cannot be over-emphasized. To have a really good set of lights can make a difference of seconds per mile in terms of your performance. I vary my set-up depending upon the rally that I am contesting. If I am driving in Yorkshire, where generally the stages are very fast and tend to have long straights, I use a concentration of up to four pencil-beam spotlights in the middle to give the maximum range. The problem with these is that they have to be set very accurately indeed. It is therefore vital that they are adjusted at night before a rally. It is worth remembering that a car tends to squat at the rear when on the move, and setting the lights when the vehicle is stationary often results in their being aimed too high.

Ideally, the middle two lamp beams should be set parallel to each other and pointing at the road surface 300 or 400 yards away. The outer two lamps should be set up at a slight divergence so that they illuminate the outer verges of the road at a similar distance. Two driving lights are also used, with their light spread to the verges about 100 yards away. These are also set a little higher than

Spectators can cause many distractions, but it is vital to treat each corner as part of a special stage and never lose your concentration.

normal, as you often find in forest rallying that you are diving into a dip and what you cannot do is see up the other side. You should avoid having the main spotlights pointing upwards, however, because if you hit any misty conditions this prevents you seeing the road completely.

On rallies in Wales and Scotland I tend to use two pencil-beam lamps in the middle and the remainder as driving lights. For twistier and slower the roads, it may be necessary to have just driving lamps in the middle and very wide spread lights on the bottom to enable you to see around corners more effectively. On narrow roads with high banks, which are usually only found on tarmac rallies, it is a good idea to cross the bottom two lamps, because by pointing the left-hand lamp to the right-hand verge the light will shine further around the corner. This will give you that little extra vision between high banks.

It is vital that when the spotlights are set up, it is done with the car fitted with the same tyres that would be used in rally conditions. Even in works teams I have found that the mechanics have fitted the wrong tyres for this purpose, where perhaps the diameter is the same all round. In a rally you may well be using a slightly larger tyre on the rear of the car which will affect the attitude of the vehicle. Likewise it is important to ensure that the quantity of fuel on board is similar to that you would use in a rally, to take a passenger with you and to make sure that the spare wheel is in place. When the lamps have been set up correctly, and I prefer to do this near to the workshop, we get the mechanics to mark the positions of the lamps on the wall to make it easier for them to set them up very close to my preference in the future.

This is all a far cry from my early days in rallying. I remember going to the Lucas Competitions Department in Oozells Street, Birmingham, to collect a 27-amp competition dynamo for my Mini. On a good night this was capable of driving four spotlights with 45-Watt bulbs, but if it was raining and it became necessary to use the windscreen wipers, you had to switch off two of the lamps as the electricity supply couldn't cope. These days, rally cars have 150-amp alternators driven by non-slip poly-V belts.

A different technique is required to drive a car quickly on an icy surface. Russell demonstrates a sideways moment on the Arctic Rally. Note the narrow tyres.

Opposite: rugged terrain and long stages made the Tour de Corse a particularly demanding event. Russell and Martin Holmes take the Escort through the Corsican countryside in 1977.

High speeds on narrow tarmac roads demand unerring commitment and concentration. Russell clinched the 1985 Open Championship after a sterling drive on the Manx International Rally.

In addition to getting the external illumination right, it is also important in darkness to ensure that the interior lights do not dazzle. Red instrument lamps are recommended as red light doesn't interfere as much with night vision as other colours. The co-driver's map lights must be arranged so that they don't distract either.

Research has shown that if you look at a bright light it takes something like 25 five minutes for your eyes to fully readjust to optimum night vision. I have often thought that it would be a good idea to wear sunglasses on road sections, right up until the point where you commence the special stage. I have attempted to do this on numerous occasions, but have found it too much of a fiddle and too uncomfortable to persist with. Someone else might like to try it.

So often people overlook the fact that the car's interior light shines directly into the driver's eyes. The first thing that happens at a stage start is that the co-driver opens the door to get his time card signed and consequently the interior light comes on, wrecking the driver's night vision. If this is the case the light should be shielded or the bulb taken out altogether.

All these little tips are very important because one of the things that has become clear to me in the past is that the more difficult the conditions, the more opportunities there are for pulling time out of other drivers. Darkness is certainly one of the major times when the difference in drivers' abilities shows through and when the care taken in preparation really pays off. You can have a situation where there is a only second or two between drivers in daylight, but during the night sections you begin to take ten or fifteen seconds a stage out of other people.

Fog and dust are probably the nastiest conditions to drive in. Fog is incredibly wearing on both driver and co-driver and very tiring on the eyes. The best way to look at fog is to realize that it is the same for everyone and is really a big opportunity to do better. To drive well in fog at night, where it undoubtedly causes most problems, one needs very good lights. The problem is how to get long-range vision in such conditions. I have found that the best fog lights are pencil beams mounted in the middle, directed at the surface of the road to the limit of your vision, be it 50 or 100 yards away.

The power of the pencil beam penetrates the fog and so you get an image of the road as far ahead as possible. This, in turn, gives you the earliest warning of corners, without there being much stray light reflecting off the fog as it does if you use headlights or driving lights. To give all-round vision closer to the car, use conventional fog lights with a sharp cut-off to the top of the beam. By running with all four lights on, maximum vision will be achieved and should the fog be exceptionally thick in patches it is possible to switch off the main lights and keep going on the fog lights. The secret is to point the main lights at the road surface fairly close in front of the car. Fog also highlights the need for a clean windscreen, again, and in fog I find that the wire elements in heated screens appear more prominent, just when you don't need any extra distraction.

It is possible to become too tense when driving in fog and concentrate on just one verge or the other when, in fact, you should force yourself to relax a little, sit back, and allow the eye to take in information from both verges. Putting the car in a higher gear also makes for more relaxed driving in fog, as using a low gear produces a stop-go throttle response which emphasizes the driver's understandable nervousness in these conditions.

The benefits of a good co-driver in foggy conditions cannot be emphasized enough. It is very useful to have someone who can read the maps well and can give you some idea as to where the road is going or has the ability to adapt the speed of pace-note reading to cope with the conditions. Fog and dust really test the precision of pace notes to the limit and it is in fog that you appreciate how important it is to have the distances written down accurately. The notional distances that some people use, which seem flexible according to the speed of the road, become useless.

If fog is likely to be encountered, the co-driver should pay extra attention to his preparation. On secret-route rallies he should measure off long straights on the map before the event and make a note on the map. He can then zero the tripmeter at the start of a straight and accurately count down the distance to go. Driving at 100mph down a straight in Dalby Forest in Yorkshire in a fog, relying on the co-driver to call the braking point, certainly gets the heart going!

If you are able to practise the rally, add prominent features to the notes that would not otherwise be read. When the Manx Rally used the main mountain roads at night, mist was a frequent hazard. We noticed that 25 yards before each corner the white line in the middle of the road usually changed from a short dash to a long dash. With this in the pace notes you can then go flat-out until you see the dashes and so leave the braking to the last minute with confidence.

My worst experience of fog came on the 1980 RAC Rally, where I was having a battle with Guy Fréquelin for third place in a Talbot. It was very foggy in Wales and we had already been off the road and damaged the lights. We arrived at the 14 or 15-mile Nant-y-Hwych stage without the lights set up correctly for fog and lost in the region of 1min 20sec to Fréquelin. He had a storming time on that one stage and put himself out of reach for the remainder of the rally.

Falling snow and dust are almost as difficult to drive in as fog, with the same problems caused by reflection from the lamps. It is important to direct the spotlights at the surface of the road in a similar way. When driving in dust, it is vital to keep as much out of the car as possible: keep the windows closed, and put the heater blower on to its maximum as it tends to pressurize the interior of the car a little and so keep out the dust.

Special stages are so short nowadays that the fatigue factor should never really enter the equation. Stages in the United Kingdom have very rarely been in excess of 30 miles and the longest I have ever known was 48 miles through the length of Dalby Forest on the John Brown RAC Rally. If you consider that a Formula 1 Grand Prix lasts one and a half hours, with the lowest average speeds over twice that achieved by a rally car, then it becomes clear that rally drivers should be able to cope easily with any fatigue which may arise.

The longest stages I have ever done on a conventional rally were on Corsica when it was held in November. There were four stages, each in the region of 120 kilometres in length, and that was quite hard going because of the tortuous nature of the roads. The Ford Escort was never the best tarmac car, and always suffered kick-back through the steering, making it a vital that you were fit and had strong arms to cope for that period of time. But those stages were exceptional. Fatigue perhaps only comes into play in very hot weather, which is something we rarely experience in Britain, although the conditions can begin to affect people on some rallies, the 1990 Welsh Rally being a classic example.

Apart from what day and night and the changing weather have to offer, the other major element with which the rally driver is in contention is the road surface. Tarmac and all the varieties of gravel provide their own problems, but winter can add to those the difficulty of deep mud or snow. The first requirement to cope with mud and surface snow is to fit narrower tyres. These cut through the surface and grip the ground beneath. Whilst I usually lean towards wider tyres to improve braking efficiency and turn in, for forest stages you also need to recognize where narrower tyres are necessary.

It is rare in the British Isles to experience continuous snow deep enough to cause severe problems. In Britain the backmarkers have an enormous advantage in snowy conditions, as the leading cars cut tram lines into the snow and eventually throw gravel and stones on to the surface which provide a lot more grip.

What faces you when driving in deep snow is that either the road has been snow-ploughed, so there is a central track of thin snow bordered by two high banks, or

'Giving it a go!' The champagne proves that it's all worthwhile: Russell and Paul White with the spoils of victory on the 1979 Manx Rally.

you have tram lines with a ridge in the middle. A lesson which needs to be learned very quickly is that you must stay in the groove and it is impossible to cut through a corner or a ridge of snow, because once the front wheels have turned into the bank at the side, the car is pulled further in. Then it is easy to find yourself with the car either buried deep in the roadside snow or spinning in the road, as I have done so often.

On the 1979 Mintex Rally I tackled the Ingleby stage in deep snow. One of the competitors ahead of me had spun in the road and I thought that it would be relatively easy to take to the snow on the verge, which was only a foot deep, and squeeze past as he was only half blocking the road. The snow pulled the car further and further in and the Escort ended up about eight or nine feet off the track. It wasn't until several other competitors had come to our assistance that we were able to continue.

It is very rarely that I have had the opportunity to drive on fully snow-ploughed roads as you see in Scandinavia, but I did contest the Arctic Rally one year. The techniques needed are very different and you tend to use very thin-section tyres with a limited number of studs. One method is to hang the tail of the car into the snowbank and use it to guide you around the corner, although I did discover that you have to be very close to the bank otherwise the tail bounces off and you end up spinning.

This is a bit like American stock car racing. I remember reading about the Darlington Oval, where the track is lined with an armco barrier. At 180mph 'the good ol' boys' put their foot on the accelerator well before the exit of the turn and the tail of the car slides out into the barrier and they get all the whitewash off the armco on the right-hand rear fender – the so called 'Darlington Stripe'. The only problem is when they are a few inches too far from the armco doing 180mph, and when the tail makes contact, it bounces back and they have a big spin!

On the Arctic Rally the temperatures were as low as minus 35 degrees Centigrade. It is necessary to wrap the entire engine up with shields and rubber sealing-strips to keep out the frost and a full-length radiator muff is used with a tiny letter-box opening. If you do go off the road and bury the car in the snowbank, the little opening can become blocked up very easily. This happened to me, and although I managed to get going again very quickly and set off down the stage, in the space of two miles the engine overheated and blew the head gasket.

One of the strange things I noticed on the Arctic Rally when it became really cold was that the grip improved quite dramatically. When the temperature is about minus 15 degrees Centigrade the level of grip is similar to that found on slippery, loose-surface roads in Britain. The ice doesn't melt under the pressure of tyres and is therefore no longer slippery.

On the Arctic Rally we had survived some problems and were forced to drive very quickly down a road section to stay on the time schedule. The Escort was running on 15-inch diameter wheels and we had the same axle ratio as we normally used with 13-inch rims. This gave the car a top speed of around 135mph and when we got up to this speed on the road section all the studs started to let go. It sounded like someone firing a machine-gun at the rear wheelarches, and when I later looked at the rear of the car there were a series of holes rather like the St. Valentine's Day Massacre!

Choosing tyres for rallying in Scandinavia is a specialist art in itself and is one which I am not versed in. Manufacturers have low-temperature rubber compounds which remains flexible even under cold conditions, but then there are is an opposing set of views which state that you should have tyres which have been studded many years before – this is believed to mature the rubber rather like a vintage wine! The rubber gradually hardens around the stud, and when you only have a limited number (approximately 110 per tyre in Finland), stud retention becomes particularly important.

There is also a theory that the hard rubber provides a sharp edge to bite into the soft, powdery snow and provide some grip because of its rigidity. The opposite approach is to run soft rubber compounds which will provide grip on hard surfaces, although this is more applicable to rallies such as the Monte Carlo where you are driving on ice rather than snow itself. It's not always easy to distinguish between the science and the black magic!

One of the most dangerous conditions I am aware of in the British Isles is patchy ice. This is particularly prevalent on the RAC Rally at night. I am always alarmed that you can be driving along very hard for a section of two or three miles without problems and suddenly come across sheet ice, particularly after the passage of, say, ten cars which glazes the surface of the road. Usually the icy section occurs where you come into a clearing and the trees no longer provide protection from the frost. I think it very worthwhile fitting a thermometer to a car for these conditions to give you some warning of frost. Even a simple paper-strip thermometer stuck on the face of the door mirror is better than nothing at all if it means that you keep a look out for the tell-tale sign, as the first bits of frost glint at you in the lights.

What I have gathered together in this chapter is really a series of hints and tips to help you to drive faster and more safely. Ultimately, though, it's up to you. The vital element for success in rallying is primarily a matter of mental approach, stimulated by a strong sense of competitiveness: at the end of the day there is no substitute for pulling your finger out and giving it a go.

9

Good cars and bad cars

The car is, of course, the most important item needed by a rally driver. Its performance and reliability can determine whether an individual even finishes a rally, let alone in what position he completes a specific event. A car needs to be competitive, reliable and powerful enough to meet the necessary requirements. Obviously final results depend to a large extent on the talents of the driver, but there are numerous instances where the car lets the driver down at the vital time. This is where development and a good deal of time-consuming behind-the-scenes work come into their own. Since the late 1960s, when I first started driving rally cars on a regular basis, I have driven all manner and forms of machinery, competitive and uncompetitive. What is perhaps most significant is how the reliability of cars has improved over the years.

Undoubtedly the Ford Sierra Cosworth is the fastest car that I have ever driven in rallies, and it is still the only machine that I have been in which gives me a thrill from its sheer straight-line speed. It is amazing what can be achieved with 300bhp! The Sierra is a very easy car to drive, in that the handling is very forgiving. It reminds me of the Vauxhall Chevette, and the weight distribution is very similar. The Ford rides bumps very well, is particularly stable because of the long wheelbase and is, in my mind, an ideal clubman's car because it flatters your performance.

My latest machine is the logical development of the Sierra Cosworth, the Sapphire Cosworth 4x4. Ford had a great opportunity to develop a four-wheel-drive car which had all the attributes of the two-wheel-drive machine plus the benefits of better traction and reduced tyre wear. Already the car shows great promise, although all the advantages haven't been transferred exactly and there are noticeable differences in the powerplant department.

To accommodate the new transmission system and to meet emission requirements, Ford revised the shape of the exhaust manifold. The result is that the new car has less power in the mid-range than its two-wheel-drive counterpart. It was mid-range torque which made the earlier Cosworth such a superb machine to drive: on many stages the level of tractability and response was such that you could exit most corners in fifth gear. That great attribute has been lost in the new car, which begins to gather momentum at about 4,500rpm but isn't on full song until 5,500 to 6,000rpm. Above that figure it delivers slightly more horsepower because the turbocharger is slightly bigger, and I'm sure careful tuning will ultimately restore the missing mid-range torque.

The 4x4 is very easy and undramatic to drive quickly for long periods. The handling is better than the two-wheel-drive version and it doesn't suffer from the excessive understeer I thought might be its bugbear. Braking is also improved: whilst the difference is not obvious on smooth roads, there is a definite advantage on, say, bumpy tarmac, where the older car would show a tendency to lock a wheel.

The advantages of the four-wheel-drive car are gained with no great weight penalty. I was surprised to discover that the Manx Rally-winning machine was only 50kg heavier than the two-wheel-drive car we had used in 1989.

Prior to the Fords, I drove the works Lancia Delta Integrale on the 1987 Lombard RAC Rally. This was certainly not the greatest car I have ever driven. It was somewhat slower than I had expected, but I could see the benefits to be gained from four-wheel drive at a time when I was campaigning a Vauxhall Astra. The Delta was very robust in design, and I feel that many of its successes can be put down to the skill of the Italian team rather than to the car's innate performance.

The Vauxhall Astra GTE comes into my category of bad cars. It was never going to be a success for GM Dealer Sport, although I did come within one second of winning the National Rally Championship in 1987. The

The Ford Sierra RS Cosworth: impressive straight line speed and forgiving handling.

Below: Russell and Neil Perkins check out the cockpit of the Sierra during a 1989 test session at Carlisle Airport.

eight-valve Astra was merely following the route pioneered by Saab in the late 1970s and its development ran into exactly the same problems as the Saab's had done in those days.

There comes a point in a front-wheel-drive car's development when you can only transmit a certain horsepower through the front wheels. After that point is reached, for every ten extra bhp the car produces, only two or three are transmitted to the road surface. The natural limit with the Astra was about 180bhp. I used Malcolm Wilson's 16-valve version of the Astra on the 1989 Mobil Rally Challenge, but found it very difficult to drive. It was very twitchy, unstable, used front tyres at an alarming rate and ultimately felt no quicker than the 185bhp eight-valve car even with 210 to 215bhp. These are just some of the big problems to be faced in front-wheel-drive rally cars.

En route to victory on the Manx, 1990. With the latest version of the Cosworth powered Sierra, Ford have added the advantages of four wheel drive while maintaining good handling.

Brookes with the loaned factory Lancia Delta Integrale he used on the 1987 Lombard RAC Rally. The car was slower than expected. Four-wheel drive was an advantage, left-hand drive a handicap.

The Opel Manta 400 was a good car, but I began to drive one in 1984, at a time when it was reaching the end of its competitive life. It rode bumps superbly well and built a reputation as being an excellent tarmac car. The handling was first rate, although it was never quite as competitive in the forests. Bearing in mind that it was up against four-wheel-drive Quattros and Metros, that was hardly surprising, however. The worst point about the Manta was the complete lack of suitable ventilation. When the lightweight panels were homologated into Group B, the team forgot to allow for the throughflow ventilation system and on the Monte Carlo Rally (the car's first international appearance) a member of the Audi team spotted this on the homologation papers. Thereafter, the vents had to be blocked off and, despite a number of tricks by the Opel team, such as having air scoops on the side windows and jacking the rear light cluster away from the body panel to enable air to flow around it, the car never had any real ventilation. This made it the most uncomfortable car to drive. I contested the Cyprus Rally in a heatwave and we attached a small strip-thermometer to the rollcage inside the car. I saw cockpit temperatures reach 150 degrees Fahrenheit. Ventilation is a point well worth considering, for there is

123

no way that a driver can perform really well in such conditions, and there is no reason why a rally car has to be totally uncivilized.

Albeit underpowered, the Vauxhall Chevette was a very good car. I drove it after a disastrous couple of seasons of unreliability with the Talbot Sunbeam Lotus, and adapted well. The Chevette was very reliable and the thought of retiring from a rally with a mechanical problem never really entered my head after a while. The mechanics at Blydenstein always turned the car out very well, and this in itself gave me additional confidence. Although it only had 245bhp, and was nowhere near the fastest car of its day, it was undoubtedly one of the best handling cars I have ever driven. It could be pushed incredibly deep into a corner, far too fast, and somehow I could always contrive to emerge from the corner on the correct line at a reasonable speed. In the majority of other machines, that sort of treatment would have meant you emerged from the corner with an enormous problem, probably 30mph slower than in a Chevette, even if you got away without having an accident.

The Vauxhall's great limitation was its 13-inch wheels, which restricted the tyre compounds it was possible to use. It was necessary to run one compound harder than the Manta over the same stages, for instance. The Chevette didn't have the straight-line speed of the Manta, either. On the last few forest rallies we overcame the problem to a degree by fitting 15-inch wheels at the back (there were body clearance problems at the front): tyre life was all but doubled and traction was improved, but by 1983 it only really made the car a better 'also ran'.

The Talbot Sunbeam Lotus was a very simple car to drive and it demonstrated its effectiveness by winning the World Rally Championship in 1981. My view will always be coloured by the fact that the ones I drove were very unreliable. The engine suffered from distortion of the block and cast aluminium sump pan. It was not uncommon to drive into parc ferme and have the crankshaft seize overnight, as the unit cooled down and twisted. The following morning you would find you couldn't turn the engine on the starter motor. On one occasion a Talbot in this state was pushed out of parc ferme and then towed behind the service car. So firmly seized was the engine that at 50mph you could drop the clutch in and the service barge would drag the car along with the rear wheels locked solid, pouring smoke off the tyres!

The Ford Escort is now a legendary machine, having achieved a longer period of sustained results than any other rally car. It was simple to drive in the forests but was never a great vehicle on tarmac surfaces. Ford tried to rectify this problem in the last two years of its competition life and the team engineer, Allan Wilkinson, spent a fortune developing tarmac versions. The ultimate derivative was christened the 'Monte Carlo car' and there were three of them, for Hannu Mikkola, Björn Waldegaard and myself.

Those really were homologation specials in the extreme. To make sure that they had the best possible weight distribution, whilst still complying with every aspect of the homologation papers, the front suspension turrets were rotated on the forward bolt so that the struts came forward by two inches. The engine could now be positioned further back in relation to the front crossmember. The bulkhead was removed and its depth reduced before it was rewelded back into the shell. In turn, this allowed the BDA engine to drop behind the front crossmember and it was mounted on outriggers on the chassis, two inches lower than normal and about

The Vauxhall Astra GTE was plagued by the inherent problems associated with powerful front wheel drive cars.

seven inches further back relative to the front wheels. Then to guarantee that the wheelbase remained the same, the rear wheelarches and axle hump were cut out and rewelded into the bodyshell two inches further forward and the axle moved forward to match.

The floorpan was cut out of the car and raised about one inch inside the bodywork so that, whilst the suspension travel was maintained, the vehicle overall was lower in relation to the wheels. The front track was four inches wider than normal Escorts and, to match this, wider rear axles were made. This enabled wheels ten inches wide to be fitted to the car. Together, these modifications gave the Escort a 45:55 weight distribution, making it very similar to a Porsche 911.

On smooth, winding tarmac this ultimate Escort had outstanding levels of roadholding, but on narrow, bumpy Irish roads it was so wide that it never truly fitted in the track and you were permanently running with the outside edges of the tyres in the loose gravel, which made it extremely difficult to drive. This car was very bad luck for me. The first event was the Circuit of Ireland Rally where both Tony Pond and myself were caught out by a bad jump. I landed on top of a dry-stone wall and badly bent the shell, to the point where the middles of the chassis rails were touching the ground. I managed to struggle out of the stage, but the vehicle was all but written off and Ford effectively washed their hands of it from then on. I argued with Allan Wilkinson that if they considered the car written off, they wouldn't mind if we had a go at repairing it ourselves.

I dragged the car up to Redditch and Allen Goodall made a superb job of straightening it, something even Ford had to give him credit for. I then contested the 24 Hours of Ypres and had another major crash when the throttle mechanism jammed. The car was running with a Kugelfischer injection system, the engine was delivering in the region of 270bhp and the rev limiter was set at 10,250rpm. This must be the ultimate revs for a rally car. We came around a very fast bend, and there was then a very short distance, about a hundred metres, to a square right-hand corner: I had to be very careful to watch my braking point. As I took my foot off the accelerator the throttle slide stuck wide open and I hit the brake pedal as hard as I could. The car spun, rolled and slid backwards, upside down along a ditch. It finally came to rest on its roof, with me still strapped in the seat with my foot clamped hard on the brake pedal. It was this alone which was stopping the engine from revving any higher. As my foot dropped off the brake pedal the engine revs climbed away until there was an enormous explosion and the unit destroyed itself. The tell-tale on the rev counter indicated that it had blown at 12,800rpm. It was, you could say, a fairly exciting machine!

As competitors in the rally were running at 30-second intervals, Paul White and I scrambled away from the car as quickly as possible in the dark. Being short, I ducked under a wire fence into the adjacent field. Paul, being somewhat taller, cocked his leg over the top. The fence was electrified, and the resulting scream could have been heard the other side of the English Channel!

The Ford was repaired again and I went off to the Ulster Rally, only to have the car aquaplane on a puddle and damage the front suspension beyond repair on a stone gate post. It finally came good on the Manx Rally – but only just. By this time it sported a revised front suspension which used a rubber-mounted compression strut. The rubbers were a standard-size component off a Granada and for some reason wore out at an alarming

The Opel Manta 400, here entertaining the spectators on the RAC Rally, gave Russell his second Open Championship title, in 1985.

'Look, no hands!' Russell makes a dramatic exit from the 1981 Circuit of Ireland. Terminal though this looks, it was in fact one of the all too infrequent occasions when the Talbot did finish a rally in Russell's hands. The service crew performed a near miracle and the team netted a third overall.

Opposite: Brookes demonstrates the opposite-lock style which helped to establish the Escort as a rallying legend. The powerful and flexible BDA engine was a major factor in its success.

Russell classes the Chevette, seen (left) in full flight on the Ulster Rally, as one of the best handling cars he has driven.

rate, leaving the suspension noticeably vague after a mere two stages. They were changed every four or five stages, and after a battle, initially with Tony Pond and then with Jimmy McRae, we ran out winners by a handful of seconds with the front wheels pointing in all directions. The only two spare sets of competition rubbers we had lasted for half the rally, but then we used another seven sets of the standard type to get to the finish. I'm sure that there were none left anywhere on the Isle of Man!

In its day the Ford Escort was the ultimate forest rally car and it achieved its record with a remarkably crude suspension set-up. I never understood what the secret of its success was. Maybe it was down to good weight distribution and preparation, but whatever the reason, the finished product was certainly more successful than its original specification would have suggested.

At the heart of a good rally car there is always a good engine. Although it was prone to blowing head gaskets if overheated, the BDA was one of the most flexible units I have ever driven. It would pull strongly from 5,000rpm and in the forests it was best to change gear at about 7,500 to 8,000rpm, so as not to break traction. The unit would happily run on to 9,000rpm, though. With an engine this high revving it was possible to fit a low-ratio final drive. 5.1:1 was normal with 13-inch wheels in the forests and

this low gearing made up for the lack of outright torque. In Corsica we used a 5.8:1 final drive, but that gave a maximum speed of only 95mph. With this engine coupled to a strong ZF gearbox and axle, we had one of the best rally cars of the day. It was let down only by the suspension when it came to tarmac stages.

The Mini was an earlier legend. Minis were always interesting machines, but they have to go into my category of bad cars. I started my rallying career in them, initially in the grossly underpowered 850 version and latterly with one of the last works engines installed for the 1971 RAC Rally. The old problems of front-wheel drive showed themselves, albeit with a mere 110bhp because of the ten-inch diameter wheels. The Mini had great difficulty in putting even this power down on to the road. This point was emphasized when I contested the Gremlin Rally in an Escort Mexico. The event finished with a series of special stages across the Epynt military ranges in Central Wales and used tests identical to those on the Boxing Day Tour of Epynt Rally which I had tackled in a Mini with an 8-port head.

In a standard Mexico all my stage times were quicker than they had been in a works Mini-Cooper S. This, in itself, gave me a clear indication of how car development had progressed in such a short time. Memories of Minis

127

The Mini, here dwarfed by the Scottish scenery in 1972, was the car which gave Russell his early introduction to international rallying. Looking back, he has mixed feelings about the famous machine.

The 'works' Austin Allegro (pictured at the start of the Tour of Dean) failed to produce a finish, but retirement was more a relief than a disappointment.

are now just a kaleidoscope of experiences. The howl of straight-cut gears; broken driveshafts on one event out of every two; the standard-diameter steering wheel required just so that you could hang on when the car was fitted with an LSD; the horrific noise in the car when it was equipped with 45DCOE Webers; tipping it on its side to change driveshafts wherever you happened to be (including the centre of Dumfries on market day with an audience of thousands); and the 'Scottish' sumpguard, essential as you sledged your way round stages on top of other people's ruts: these are just a few of my memories of the Mini. Why did we ever rally them!

Probably the lemon amongst all the cars I have driven was the works Skoda 1000MB, which had the supreme homologation feature of the 'Mountain Gearbox Ratios'. At 6,000rpm it had a top speed of 72mph, while acceleration was definitely measured in terms of days and hours rather than seconds, and reliability was non-existent!

Equal first in the lemon stakes was a 'works' Austin Allegro 1300. It had all the bad attributes of a Mini, a very cammy engine which delivered no power under 5,500rpm

and ran out of steam at 7,500rpm, and excessive torque-steer from the front suspension which was not sorted correctly. In addition, it suffered from appalling squat, dip, dive and other problems related to the hydrolastic suspension. I was relieved when a driveshaft broke half-way through the Tour of Dean and we were able to retire to the Speech House for a quick drink.

Another of my worst rallying experiences came in a Group 1 RS2000 I used in the Philippines. It was built by the local dealer and I was co-driven by Ho Puay Koon. Although the machine itself wasn't too bad, the standard of rally mechanicing had to be seen to be believed. We had a service crew totalling 22: four of them were in an Escort saloon, seven were in a wrecker truck with a crane on the back, and the other eleven were in a Transit van, leaving very little room for spares! There was one good mechanic in the whole bunch, called Brofar, but they fixed him very elegantly at the first service point when he was changing a shock absorber. Someone trod on his hand and broke his fingers. We then lost the entire service crew for a day and a half, which was the best thing

Russell sees the Peugeot 309GTI as a possible class winner, but was not impressed with its overall performance when he drove an example on the 1989 Mobil Challenge.

The Toyota Celica GT4, here in the hands of Jimmy McRae, was another car Russell had the opportunity to drive on the 1989 Mobil Challenge. Good traction and handling helped to make it easy to drive.

that ever happened, and we progressed well to the twelve-hour half-way halt at Baguio.

In the regulations it stated that you were able to take the car out of parc ferme for one hour, work on it and put it back afterwards. As some of the management staff were present we assumed that everything would be handled correctly. But when we got in for the restart we realised that things had gone disastrously wrong. The team had incurred 59 minutes of road penalties out of our one-hour maximum, before we had even started the second half of the rally: obviously they had misunderstood the regulations and had kept the car out of parc ferme beyond the permitted hour, although the only major item of work was to stop the exhaust pipe knocking on the bodywork.

Fortunately we were delayed for an hour on the start ramp for the second half, because the local mayor had decided to hold a parade in conjunction with the rally and we had to wait until the band had finished marching up and down. Under the cover of darkness I took the opportunity to look around the car and shone the torch underneath. They had certainly fixed the exhaust alright! It was obvious that a couple of the mechanics had hung on to the tail pipe, stretched the mounting rubbers to keep the exhaust away from the bodywork, and then tied it to the axle with a tow rope.

There was one strange mechanic who, despite our wishes and the best intentions of the interpreter, thought that his job was to check all the hose clips. At the first service point all 22 mechanics decided to work on the engine. When we dragged them all off, we found this one man busily undoing every hose clip. I brought the interpreter over, questioned him as to why he was doing this, and he replied that he had been allocated the job of checking the hose clips, and therefore by undoing them and doing them up again he was checking to ascertain that they were in order. When we left parc ferme I

noticed that petrol was pouring everywhere. A quick check revealed that every hose clip on the car, including those on brake fluid and water pipes, was undone. I spent the next half an hour fastening every jubilee clip in sight. And so it went on – not my greatest rallying experience!

Back in Britain, in happier circumstances, the televised Mobil Challenge in 1989 was an excellent opportunity to drive a variety of cars. Two of these were the Peugeot 309 GTI and the Vauxhall Astra GTE and they confirmed my aversion to front-wheel drive. They were just as difficult to drive as the Mini was in my early career and, quite frankly, didn't make any sense at all in rally terms, except as possible class winners.

Although the four-wheel-drive Toyota Celica was only a practice machine built for Leif Asterhag, it was impressively quick, extremely easy to drive and handled very well, albeit a little tail happy. With some attention to detail in the direction of the suspension and the torque split, this could be cured very easily. It was amazing that one could get in the car for the first time and almost instantly record very fast stage times with confidence. The gearbox was a delight, the engine gave a lot of torque and to someone who was accustomed to driving a two-wheel-drive car it was a revelation to experience how quickly it left the start line on the loose.

The BMW M3 was something of a surprise. Ostensibly it was of a similar specification to the one which Patrick Snijers had used to win the 1988 Manx Rally, although the car felt extremely nervous, jumped about excessively on bumpy tarmac and appeared to have been set up with a full race suspension. In addition, there seemed to be a lot of feedback through the steering. All these factors made it extremely tiring to drive, even though I only used the car on short stages. The M3 didn't inspire confidence on narrow bumpy roads and if this was the car which Snijers used to win the Manx, I take my hat

Walter Röhrl, seen here, was one of the few people to get somewhere near taming the ferocious short wheelbase Audi Quattro S2. In private testing, Russell found it shatteringly quick.

off to him. He must have been a very brave man.

The one big regret in my rallying career is that I never had the opportunity to drive one of the Group B 'supercars' in anger before they were banned. I did do some testing at Vallelunga with Audi, using the early Quattro, and that showed me the potential that was on offer. More recently, at a private test session, I was able to drive Walter Röhrl's Quattro S2, which is now privately owned.

Although it was running on a relatively low boost, so that it 'only' gave in the region of 500bhp, it was shatteringly quick and one could appreciate that it would be extremely difficult to drive for any length of time. Its performance figures included acceleration from rest to 100mph in five seconds, which was way beyond the realms of anything else I have ever driven.

More recently I have driven the Ford Sierra 2.9i XR4x4. In many ways this car has been an eye opener, and I cannot understand why Ford didn't develop it for rallying several years ago alongside the Sierra Cosworth. After just three events it was quite clear that the car could have been quicker than the Cosworth in the forests. Potentially, it could make a very good clubman's car, too. The V6 engine, with its cast-iron block, must be very reliable and I would envisage no problems or rebuilds throughout a whole season of rallying. It handles as well as any car I have ever driven, is very safe, rides the bumps well and is easy on tyres. I could anticipate using a mere eight to twelve tyres on a Scottish Rally, for example. Now that the engine management system has been sorted, it will undoubtedly be quicker than it was earlier in 1990.

Probably the most interesting vehicle I have driven was a MAN 6x6. The turbo wastegate was screwed down so that it gave around 350bhp, but the performance was hardly electrifying as it had seven tons of spares on board and the gross vehicle weight was 22 tons, including fuel. It handled remarkably well and on certain desert stretches

it was possible to get it into a six-wheel drift around some of the long corners. Despite all the punishment we gave it during the Paris–Dakar Raid, including hitting a washaway at fairly high speed, which was sufficient to bend the front axle quite substantially, nothing major ever went wrong. That was probably just as well – I began to understand the problems that mechanics can have when I attempted a routine shock-absorber change at the half-way halt. It took two of us to pull the component off its mountings and carry it.

The vehicle had an uncanny ability to climb sand dunes and steep gradients. It had a seven-speed gearbox, of which first gear was effectively a crawler, and then two overall transfer ratios, in addition to a facility which enabled you to lock the centre differential and both front and rear differentials. This gave the vehicle numerous permutations of available drive systems.

One of the problems of travel in the Sahara Desert is that the wind blows from north to south every day and consequently the sand dunes (or barcânes) build up like waves. The north faces are gently sloping, but the south faces have vertical drops. This doesn't present a problem when travelling from east to west because you tend to thread your way between the dunes, but one special stage, from an oasis called Bilma to Zoo Baba, went directly from north to south.

Everyone viewed this stage with great trepidation, as we were to be the first wheeled vehicles to cross this section of desert since a Citroën expedition in 1949. The organizers had devised the route in a helicopter and the course was littered with high sand dunes. The technique was to charge the sand dune in an attempt to make it to the top. If you didn't reach the highest point it was necessary to deflate all the tyres and run them at about eight pounds per square inch pressure. You then had to select a crawler gear and low transfer, in the hope that the truck would grind its way to the top of even a near-vertical cliff.

It was absolutely critical to attack the sand dunes at right angles, for as soon as you tried to drive across the face of the dune the cab would gradually start to point downhill no matter how much steering lock was applied. I was very fortunate to get away with this manoeuvre once, as we saw many trucks lying irretrievably on their sides during the stage. After that one fright I was very careful how we approached the dunes for the rest of the journey.

Having reached the highest point, it was then necessary to survey the scene, because very often the vertical drop the other side was in the region of 80 or 90 feet. It was then vital that if you reached the bottom, you were not faced immediately with another dune which you couldn't climb without a run at it. Many vehicles retired on this section because they couldn't get up a subsequent sand dune. If it was safe to descend, the technique was not to put it in a crawler gear, but to use fifth or sixth to avoid over-revving the engine. That way, you hit the bottom of the drop with the front wheels turning, which pulled the nose out so that the truck didn't nosedive. You then kept going for a couple of hundred yards to leave the sand dune before beginning the painful process of having to inflate the tyres again. We did this about twenty times on one special stage of 185 miles. That one section took eighteen hours.

On that stage in particular I was thankful that we had a reliable vehicle. We were somewhat better off than one sister truck, as it had suffered a bent front propshaft in an accident. To make any speed the crew had to remove the shaft, and then refit it to crawl up every dune. The threads on the bolts must have been nearly worn out with the number of times the shaft had been taken off and refitted!

It is good to have a sense of humour in these circumstances. During this stage the gearbox had broken on the Astra 4S and, whilst waiting for the trucks to pass, Guy Colsoul and Alain Lopez had taken off the one-piece glassfibre front section of the car. They had obviously seen us coming and when we arrived on the scene there were Guy and Alain, steering wheel in their hands, crash helmets on, sitting behind the bonnet and wings, with no car in sight, behaving like a couple of madmen. At first we thought the sun had got to them!

A Paris–Dakar effort like GM's costs a fortune, but rallying is not all big-budget works teams by any means. I once had the opportunity to drive a Davrian, an early ancestor of the Darrian glassfibre kit car which is now campaigned successfully by a number of clubmen in Britain. I was asked to go along to Tregaron in Central Wales to assist with testing and I must admit that I was pleasantly surprised with what I discovered. The vehicle was so light that even a relatively low-powered engine gave it a good deal of acceleration. By having the engine over the driven wheels the traction was superb and I felt at that stage that it would become a very good car and certainly one which I would recommend.

It's all a matter of defining your aims and making the best use of what's available. For at the end of the day there is no doubt which is the best rally car: it's the one that wins rallies.

10

It's tough at the top

My career has spanned nearly three decades and right from my early days in rallying I have been fortunate to compete against some of the world's finest drivers. I have learned many vital lessons from other competitors and I can recall many occasions where I witnessed, first hand, some of the greatest performances by other people. Over the years I have come to respect many competitors, but of the thousands of drivers I have rallied against, a handful really stick in my mind because of their driving brilliance.

One of the great drivers who was competing at the time when I really got going in rallying was Timo Mäkinen – a legendary name among rally drivers. He was very aggressive and had a large personality which he imposed wherever he went. He wasn't averse to a tipple to boost his performances either!

One of the special things about competing on the RAC Rally between 1968 and 1970 was that although I was a complete outsider, the nature of the sport meant that it was possible for me to compete against the likes of Timo. I had this tremendous feeling of privilege about being able to rally over the same stages as him. Certainly this is an experience which very few racing drivers will ever have, because it is very rare for today's top Formula 1 drivers, for example, to compete in anything outside their own championship. The fact that a relative beginner can take part in the same events as the established stars is something which rallying should go out of its way to preserve.

I felt it was a great shame that Timo's last years in the sport lacked a feeling of good grace. We all have to face the fact that young drivers will come and challenge our position and take over from us, but Timo was never prepared to accept this. Perhaps that was one of the reasons why he was so competitive. Even on an RAC Rally when he was driving very slowly indeed, he was well known for going out of his way to baulk people and stop them passing. His reputation deserved far more in terms

of his attitude late in his career.

I've often tried to determine why you begin to drive slower as you grow older. The obvious reasons are that you are less physically active, your reactions are slower and your eyesight begins to deteriorate. These factors have a part to play of course, but I think that the real reason is something more than that. To drive competitively there needs to be a desire to beat other people, and when you are starting out in the sport that competitive element is fresh and pushes you on to drive harder.

There have been quite a few instances where drivers have kept this competitive edge relatively late in life but this is often when they have entered the sport at a late stage.

The classic example is Fangio, who was one of the greatest *rally* drivers ever. The inter-city races he used to contest in South America were exactly like long-distance special-stage rallies as we know them today. He moved on to participate in European Formula 1 racing at the age of 38, and continued to dominate the scene for a period of ten years. He was not driving any slower at that point in his career, but reckoned that the desire, not the physical ability, to succeed and win races had largely deserted him when he eventually retired. This illustrates my belief that lack of stimulus is one of the major factors which can adversely affect someone's performance. For this reason it is vital that an individual introduces variety into the type of rallies he contests. This in itself can stoke up the desire to succeed again.

The other aspect is a basic human factor: the older a person becomes the more they will try to cheat death and extend life. A young person arguably has the most to gain from staying alive, because of the full life in front of him, but young people rarely consider death. The instinct for self-preservation definitely creeps in when you reach the age of 40 or so, and this will affect the driving style. I admit that I drive more cautiously than I did in my

earlier career. But in rallying this can often pay dividends because the youngster often throws the car off the road in a silly accident while the older driver goes on to win the event by not making a mistake.

One of my biggest regrets is that my rally career was progressing at the time when Roger Clark had been at the top of the sport in this country for ten years. His performances in World and British Championship rallies were legendary, but Ford, as they have so often done, set Roger up to be Aunt Sally, unfortunately in a very negative way – 'If you beat Roger Clark then maybe you are going somewhere' might have been all right, but the attitude seemed to be rather 'If you can't even beat Roger then you're not worth a light,' which demeans the principal driver.

I felt that I was the young man of the moment and it was on the 1976 Scottish Rally that I beat him and earned the works drive. I feel regretful about this because Roger deserved better treatment and more recognition from Ford than he actually received at that point. He is his own man and continued in rallying for a considerable time afterwards: he still enjoyed the sport – his recent participation in historic rallying shows that he still does – and I am quite sure that he took the attitude that he was

Russell and Roger Clark share a joke during the 1989 Lombard RAC Rally.

damned if anybody was going to tell him when to retire and he would give up rallying when he wanted to and at a time of his own choosing.

Roger went on to drive for R-E-D, the team which I am now involved with, on the 1980 RAC Rally, where he was partnered by television personality Chris Searle. This made one of the most memorable programmes in Searle's series, In at the Deep End – all the other programmes involving Searle and his colleague Chris Heiney revolved around the 'Oh, didn't he do well under the circumstances and hasn't he learnt quickly!' theme. The one with Roger was totally different because he hadn't lost the competitive element and he dearly wanted to win the RAC Rally. Searle was undoubtedly in the way, Roger let him know in no uncertain terms and it made a television programme which had far more bite to it than others in the series. The look on Roger's face when he explained to the cameras how Searle had wrong-slotted him up the motorway and they had consequently lost road time summed up the whole series!

It is this independent aspect of Roger's personality which has made him such a popular competitor, particularly with clubmen and spectators. It is well known that only on rare occasions will he stand up and make speeches on behalf of motor clubs. He hasn't been involved with the RAC and the governing of the sport – he has always 'done it his way.' The apparently arrogant and aggressive manner he showed in the early days is probably a major reason why he has been so successful. He is certainly often regarded as the individual who stuck two fingers up to everyone!

Of all British drivers in recent years Tony Pond is

Roger Clark on his way to victory on the 1972 RAC Rally.

undoubtedly the man who attracted the most attention. Certainly he was offered the best opportunities, most of which, however, ended prematurely. His involvement with the Austin Rover Metro 6R4 was a case in point. That was a great pity for British rallying, for John Davenport's greatest achievement was to persuade the only major British-owned car company to become involved in rallying at the highest level, in a project which, had it not taken quite as long to come to fruition, would arguably have been immensely successful. Despite all the things which have since happened to John Davenport, the opportunities this project gave to British drivers to compete in World Championship events at the time shouldn't be overlooked. Had there been an ongoing development programme for the Metro, I am sure we would have seen more from the Abingdon factory.

That Metro programme reflects what has so often happened in Tony Pond's career. Whilst we were both rallying well before the Mexico Championship, it was that series which brought us both to prominence, Tony in 1972 when he finished second to Will Sparrow and myself in 1973. Tony took a Scottish Rally appearance as his prize drive and was rewarded with a much-publicized top-ten finish. He was subsequently involved with the Opel Group 2 Ascona, British Leyland's TR7, Talbot's new Sunbeam and Nissan with the 160J, but all these programmes were with teams close to being competitive without ultimately achieving world-class success. This is one of the greatest pities in Pond's career; he has never quite been able to find himself in a fully-competitive car at the right time.

One wonders whether that was because of circumstances that were forced upon him, which I recognize can happen, or whether at certain critical times in his career he felt the attraction of the money was stronger than that of the more competitive car. He has undoubtedly been the quickest British driver I have ever been up against, and I feel that his talent and ability ultimately deserved better.

One of the competitors I have been most involved with is Jimmy McRae, who came into the sport relatively late, having been involved in motorcycle scrambling. He didn't actually take part in any rallies until the mid-1970s. A very difficult person to compete against, Jimmy's great attribute has been his reliability.

The driver for whom I had the highest regard, because in his field he seemed to be pre-eminent, was Walter Röhrl. Walter would never pretend to be a top-class secret route rally driver, and the number of crashes he had on the RAC Rally proves this point, but he was superb on pace notes. Never in my presence did he criticize the secret rallying side of the sport, however. He just accepted that it existed and it was something that he wasn't very good at. I first met him on the 1977 Hunsrück Rally, which I tackled with Peter Bryant. We had a rally-long battle against Walter who was driving a Fiat 131 Abarth. Although we led for part of the rally, the result was very much on a knife edge because pace notes were not permitted and it was my first time over in Germany. Eventually we lost out when I tipped the Ford on its side and dropped to third overall.

A rare photograph of the entire Ford team assembled to tackle the Lombard RAC Rally. From left to right in the front row are David Richards, Ari Vatanen, Peter Ashcroft, Hans Thorzelius, Björn Waldegaard, Arne Hertz, Hannu Mikkola, Russell Brookes and Paul White.

There were times on pace-note rallies where Walter could turn in staggering performances. This proved totally demoralizing to the opposition. On the Ulster Rally in 1984 he entered an Audi Sport Quattro, undoubtedly the quickest machine on the entry list, but nevertheless very difficult to drive. He selected his stages, and it seemed obvious when he was going to tear the opposition apart, just by watching his level of concentration change as he composed himself before a test on which he was going to put in maximum effort.

On a Portugal Rally one year he turned in an absolutely stunning performance. He identified a group of stages in the Arganil area where there was a likelihood of fog and spent an enormous amount of time practising those tests so that he knew them by heart. On the event itself there was fog and Walter was able to put up times which put him out of reach of the rest of the field. It is performances like those which set him apart from other drivers. Significantly, he is one of very few rally drivers who have succesfully made the transition to motor racing.

When I first started out in the sport back in the 1960s the driver whom I really admired was Vic Elford. He was

my hero – and arguably the greatest British rally driver ever, yet he never achieved the level of publicity associated with, say, Roger Clark and Paddy Hopkirk. Paddy's media attention came primarily as a result of his victory on the Monte Carlo Rally, and yet Vic also won the Monte, in a Porsche. He was one of the few British drivers who ever succeeded with foreign teams.

Vic had quite an unusual start in rallying, in that originally he was a co-driver: he became a works co-driver for the Ford Motor Company, partnering Brian Melia. The latter was unable to contest some stages on the Acropolis Rally through illness and the pair swapped seats. Vic was quicker than Brian and they duly exchanged roles from then on. Vic went on to do so much more outside rallying. He had a career in Formula 1 racing, which included a third overall at the French Grand Prix at Rouen, but he is perhaps best known for some brilliant performances in Porsche racing sports cars, including the famous Targa Florio which he won in 1968. These feats mark him out as a driver of outstanding talent.

Three Finnish drivers with whom I have come into contact during my involvement in rallying, particularly in

138

Ari Vatanen, pictured in the Rothmans Escort, was capable of putting in some staggering stage times even in his early career.

the late 1970s, were Hannu Mikkola, Ari Vatanen and Pentti Airikkala. They have very different characters, but all three have the same competitive Finnish edge. Hannu was at the absolute peak of his abilities at the end of the 1970s, although it should not be forgotten that he passed through an incredibly low period in his career in the middle of the decade when, having lost his Ford works drive, he scratched around without success before embarking on a year with Toyota in 1977. This was followed by a Ford drive again in '78 and '79. I am sure that the interim period added an extra degree of determination to his will to succeed.

Smooth driving was one of Hannu's talents. Although I have only really witnessed his driving style from the queue to start a special stage, it was very noticeable that his Escort was never more sideways than absolutely necessary and his driving always seemed to be undertaken in an incredibly relaxed manner. This outward calm

meant he came across to the world at large as one of rallying's gentlemen, but under the skin he was still the hard-edged Finn and it is that competitive element which made him so successful.

On the Scottish Rally in 1978 we came to a group of three stages in the Glenshellish area, where Hannu was first on the road, Markku Alèn was second in the Fiat 131 and I was about 30 seconds behind Hannu in the results. The surface of the tests was very soft and it was widely known that being first or second on the road offered quite an advantage. Alèn sustained a puncture, and we eased into the time control at the stage arrival on our minute. When Markku arrived with the boot of his car still open he was able to collect the time he wanted but had to start the test third on the road.

At the end of the stage there was a wait of around five minutes in the forest until we commenced the subsequent test. Hannu sat before the arrival control and we parked

Pentti Airikkala's finest hour yet came with his victory on the 1989 Lombard RAC Rally in a Mitsubishi.

behind him. Then Markku arrived and had a brief conversation with Hannu. To our surprise, the latter didn't move into the time control as his minute arrived. It got to the point where we were due to enter the control and we reversed in order to drive around Hannu: at the same time he began to back up, so blocking our passage to the time control. Consequently, Alèn was in a position to come through and enter the control a minute ahead of his due time, without penalty. Markku then did one stage first on the road, with Hannu second and me third, before they reverted to the original positions on the next stage. I was immensely angry at this and rose to the bait with some stupid driving and slid off the road for five minutes on that next stage – it had certainly proved how the Finns stick together.

Hannu must be unique in that he has had no job in life other than driving rally cars. He received notification of his final college examination results whilst he was driving a works Volvo on the Acropolis Rally! Although he trained as an engineer, he never actually took up a position in the trade and has remained a professional rally driver ever since.

Ari Vatanen was a driver I got to know quite well at the start of his career, initially when he drove an Opel Kadett on a number of rallies in Britain, and then when he was given amazing opportunities to drive works Ford Escorts. The latter offer came at a time when any other driver would have been scratching about, trying to get established. Ford were very perceptive, for Ari turned out to be one of the world's greatest rally drivers, winning his World Championship in 1980 in a David Sutton Escort. Although he did have a surprising number of crashes, Ari was a very difficult competitor to beat when he did stay on the road for his stage times were quite exceptional and this was very daunting for other competitors, especially when he was only in his early twenties.

I have competed against 'The British Finn' – Pentti Airikkala – on numerous occasions. He has always seemed to be the black sheep in the Finnish family of great rally drivers, and many of his fellow countrymen seem antagonistic towards him. His rallying has suffered because of this, but there is no disputing that he is an extremely aggressive competitor and on occasions has allowed his aggressiveness to stray beyond the bounds of normal acceptability in terms of his relationships with other people. I got to know Pentti very well during the 1977 Open Championship when we had a year-long battle. One of the most surprising things I discovered about him, which holds true to this day, is that when he is driving a car which the pundits say is the most competitive and the best for the event he turns in a relatively poor performance. Whenever he has a car in which he is seen to be the underdog, he does remarkably well and can often win rallies.

It was like that with the Vauxhall Chevette, which was known to be a fast car in 1977 but was still in the early stages of its development. It was believed to be very good on tarmac and not so competitive in the forests but, with

a couple of exceptions, Pentti's results tended to be the other way around. So often it seemed that on tarmac rallies he would push too hard and suffer the consequences.

I was delighted when he won the RAC Rally in 1989, possibly because he is of a similar age to myself and the feeling that one of the old firm could still win the rally did wonders for my confidence. I wished him every success with the new Ford car. It was a deal which he richly deserved after a lot of hard effort, during a career which hasn't always given him the breaks a number of other Finnish competitors have received.

There was a period during which Finnish rally drivers were exceptionally successful, but they now seem to be challenged by mainland European drivers. I've thought about the reasons for the Finnish success long and hard in the past and have never really come to any firm conclusions. Finland is a small country with a population of only four million or so, but it is an incredibly sport-conscious place. Over the years, they have produced champions in greater numbers than any statistics of population would suggest they should, and not just in rallying. Undoubtedly, the weather conditions and roads in Finland provide budding rally drivers with exactly the right sort of experience on suitable terrain from an early

Opposite: Carlos Sainz, World Rally Champion in 1990, hails from Spain. He won the 1990 RAC Rally with a very impressive drive, while no Finns featured in the results, exemplifying the way Southern European drivers have emerged in recent years to challenge the long-time Scandinavian dominance.

Russell believes that Louise Aitken-Walker, first Ladies World Champion, has not yet had the opportunity to develop her talent to the full.

Michèle Mouton was capable of beating all comers. Her great rally career reached its peak in the Audi Quattro.

141

age, but I suspect that the reason for their sucsess also has to do with the national temperament of the country.

For a long time Finland was subjected to Swedish or Russian domination and has only been an independent country since the early part of this century. As with all new countries, there is a strong national assertiveness and this spills over into the area of sport, where Finnish competitors have a hardness and a competitive determination which we often lack in this country.

It might be coincidence, but the wane of the almost total Finnish dominance of rallying does seem to date from Henri Toivonen's fatal crash in 1986. Until that point, Finnish drivers had a feeling almost of invincibility which permeated everything they did and conditioned their attitude to the sport. The incident in Corsica shattered this belief and seems to have affected the performance of the majority of Finnish drivers ever since. It is quite surprising even now that when you get into conversation with rallying Finns in general, almost invariably within the space of five minutes the discussion turns to the subject of Henri's death.

With the Finnish influence in decline, one of the biggest trends in recent years has been the move to recruiting Latin drivers. This is part of the recognition by motor manufacturers in southern Europe that rallying is important. In their home lands Carlos Sainz, Massimo Biasion, Didier Auriol and Alessandro Fiorio are very well known people, and it is that publicity which has provided the interest and the incentive in those countries to continue to promote the sport. It is similar to the situation which existed in Finland in the late 1970s, when rallying achieved the level of media attention which would be reserved for football in the British Isles.

Conversely, the way publicity affects rallying has played a part in one of the greatest disappointments for British rallying, the career to date of Louise Aitken-Walker. I was a judge at the Ford Fiesta 'Find a Lady Driver' Challenge, when Louise first competed, and it was immediately obvious that she had a lot of talent. She entered the Challenge without holding a driving licence but passed her test almost straight away after she had placed an entry. It became quite clear to all the judges that she was going to emerge in the top three, even when there were still over five hundred contestants to vet.

It is a shame that her career has never finally fulfilled the promise it showed in those early days. A great mistake has been made by team managers putting her in cars which are less than competitive. Talbot, General Motors and Ford all gave way to the temptation to use the fact that she was a lady to create publicity for a car which was otherwise uncompetitive, without allowing Louise to realize her own true potential. She really needed a team to place her in a conventional, easy to drive motor car and she would have become a driver as great in stature as Michèle Mouton, capable of beating all comers.

In 1985, Louise drove a Nissan 240RS. On the Scottish Rally, where Mike Broad and myself were in an Opel Manta, she set some excellent stage times despite losing time early on through punctures. It was around the half-way point when Mike pointed out to me that Louise had been matching some of our stage times and had beaten us on a handful, in a car which was nearing the end of its competitive life and was not as fast as the Manta. That competitive edge was still there when she drove a 1,600cc Peugeot 205 in 1987, frequently matching and beating Malcolm Wilson in the 1,900cc version. But recently the potential seems to have been lost because Louise has continued to drive non-competitive two-wheel drive rally cars for the last decade – and eventually that would knock the stuffing out of anybody.

She is definitely the case which disproves the rule, in that being a lady has been a great disadvantage to her career. Even after her best drives, team managers continued to say 'Didn't she do well...for a lady', when, in fact, her abilities would have stood her in good stead against any drivers in Britain. It indicates perhaps the limited outlook of those team managers in the United Kingdom who have competitive cars, that the tremendous opportunities she presents have not been seized. There may still be time to rectify the situation.

11

Memories

In the course of twenty years in the top flight of British rallying I have competed in a lot of rallies, and each event has added something important to the memories I cherish. I have rallied in many corners of the globe, and it isn't always the details of the specific event which stick most firmly in my mind, more the people, the scenery and the type of terrain. In this chapter I have gathered together some of the most vivid recollections.

Of all the memories, those of the Paris–Dakar Raid are among the most powerful and will always stay with me. One of the great eye-openers was the experience of travelling through destitute countries on this event, and it highlighted our privileged position. We were in a truck which cost about £100,000, with £30–40,000 in spares on board and £20,000 in a cash safe welded to the chassis rail, passing through some of the poorest areas in the world.

I still sometimes find myself wondering whether it's really right morally for the Paris–Dakar Rally to pass through this region, exciting and challenging though it is as a motoring adventure. After thinking long and hard, I come to the conclusion that if the event didn't exist the people who live there certainly would be no better off: on the positive side, not only does the passage of the event bring entertainment into their lives, but it does a little good for the local economy and, perhaps most important, it does help to bring the problems of the Third World to the attention of outsiders.

The contrast in life styles was brought home to me at the first fuel dump. The first section of the rally down to Tammanrasset was a series of loops off the main road where there were fuel stations, but as the rally headed further south there were none, and the organisers had arranged fuel dumps in the desert. We found a bivouac at the end of each section and the mechanics set about working on the vehicles. As I wasn't a mechanic I drew the short straw and was sent to buy some fuel. I negotiated with the local trader to buy my two 45-gallon drums of diesel, for which I paid 8,000 francs (£800). The next problem was to have the fuel pumped into the vehicle with a hand-operated pump we carried on board.

Six of the locals fulfilled the task without further ado, but I was then faced with the problem of not knowing what to pay them. I went to the safe in the truck and took out the smallest-denomination note I had – 10 francs. I gave this to the man I took to be the head pumper, not knowing the problems that it would cause. About five minutes later, as I was packing up the truck, a huge fight started, with rocks flying around and people getting struck over the head with sticks. There was blood everywhere, so I hastily decided to jump in the truck and drive away, without really understanding what it was all about.

The next day I had to get some fuel again from another dump and once more found a local trader, paying him about 10,000 francs for the fuel. This time the man spoke reasonable French and I asked him if he could find some pumpers for me. He went off, returned with a group and they set to work.

Then I asked him how much money I should pay them. 'Twenty centimes,' he replied. I dived into my pocket and realized I hadn't enough change for twenty centimes each, but he looked and told me it was enough: I was supposed to pay the pumpers two or three centimes each! I suddenly realised why there had been a fight the previous evening.

One of the things which amazed me about the Paris–Dakar was the enthusiasm that Tony Fall (GM's rally boss) had for the event. It would have been very easy for him to stand back, fly around the route and avoid the strain and discomfort, but that was not how he chose to do it. In fact, Tony's enthusiasm became very wearing for the mechanics, as he tried to get them to do physical jerks after three nights without sleep. He was always involved

Russell, flanked by Andy Schultz and Ronnie Gardsfeldt, poses in front of the MAN 6x6 which Opel used as a support vehicle for the 1986 Paris–Dakar Rally.

The other side of the fence: a driver rarely experiences life from the mechanic's end of the sport, but Russell acclimatizes to his new career prior to leaving for the Sahara.

and appeared to have as much energy after 27 days as he did after day one. I was very impressed with that.

I've always had a soft spot for the old style Circuit of Ireland, rallies which always had a certain special quality. Malcolm Neill's last event, with 610 stage miles, was a fabulous endurance rally. I feel that the competitiveness and involvement amongst competitors is diminished on today's shorter events. There isn't much that the organizers can do about it because of FISA's regulations, but I am disappointed that Malcolm has been forced to move away from that old spirit with the recent changes to the RAC Rally.

It has now been changed dramatically from its traditional secret route formula, which used to be one of the hallmarks of the RAC. In 1990 it has effectively become the Tour of Yorkshire and Southern Scotland. This will be a great loss, as it is no longer truly the RAC Rally of Great Britain, and I feel that the organizers must tread very carefully, or the event may lose its special flavour and appeal, which could lead to its demotion from the World Championship.

Some of the most interesting special stages that I've ever done were on the Bahrain Rally, which I tackled with Mike Broad in one of Mike Little's Talbot Sunbeams. The outing was very successful in that we beat the Qatari Saeed Al Hajri in the Rothmans Porsche 911 into second place. Practising the route was permitted, which was quite a privilege because most of the island was closed off. The southern sector was the private reserve of the State ruler. We successfully found our way around the majority of the special stages, but were reading the road book down one particular section of well-defined track when it disappeared into the sea. We stopped, turned around, retraced our path and checked all the junctions off the road books in case we had made a mistake, before reaching the conclusion that we were on the correct path

where the road entered the sea.

At that moment one of the Arab drivers in a Toyota came charging past, dived straight into the sea and calmly drove for three-quarters of a mile with the water reaching eighteen inches up the side of the vehicle. Mike and I were quite staggered at this. The first task was to decipher which path should be taken through the water, as the Toyota driver hadn't followed a straight line. We tried to drive alongside the track because, although the road was only six inches below the level of the surrounding sand, the water came a fair way up because of the flatness of the terrain. But that put us in danger of having to abandon our vehicle, a Daihatsu truck, because the sand became very soft indeed as we neared the water's edge. I managed to keep the vehicle moving across the track by turning it in circles, but eventually we got bogged down in the sand with the tide coming in. It took around two hours to extract our truck, and this was only done by jacking the machine up in the baking sun, putting our head and arms under the water until the jack was under the axle and lifting it sufficiently to enable driftwood to be placed under the wheels. After that, we took the spark plugs out and crawled the vehicle out on the starter motor (remember *Ice Cold in Alex*?).

It was then that one of the Arab drivers explained the procedure for crossing the water. It was vital that you stayed on the track, as it was made up of much harder sand than the surrounding ground. Even in the sea the track remained hard. The idea was to traverse the section at just the right speed so that you didn't create a bow-wave ahead of the vehicle. It was then possible to peer through the crystal-clear sea water and see the slightly darker sand of the track. By not straying from this it was possible to cross the water without sinking. But if you strayed a foot either side of the track, the vehicle would be stuck irretrievably.

The regulations for the Paris–Dakar meant that the MAN truck had to run as a competing vehicle, but its real purpose was to support the Astra 4S. Guy Colsoul and Alain Lopez are here seen on the prologue stage of the event.

One of the special stages on the event took place near high tide and had probably the most amazing pace notes we have ever written for a rally: 'At the end of the Ra's al Barr section, aim at the light beacon three-quarters of a mile away across the bay'. Something like thirty or forty cars were abandoned on this section as they drifted off the side of the track. After the passage of two or three cars the water became very muddy and it was no longer possible to make out the outline of the darker sand. By running at number two we had a tremendous advantage – but it still made for an exciting rally.

I savour many pleasant memories from my time in the Middle East, but I also had one of the most frightening experiences of my life during practice for the Bahrain Rally. Coming back from the desert one evening, after practising in a Mitsubishi Colt 1300, we eventually rejoined the dual carriageway back to the capital city of Manama and sat at the first traffic island waiting while an innocent looking Mercedes 250 Diesel went around the roundabout and headed off down the road. The car appeared quite ordinary, with an Arab driver and no unusual markings.

About five minutes later we caught the car and passed it, not for one minute considering that we had done anything unusual. I then noticed that the driver was blowing his horn furiously, flashing his lights and all the time moving towards our car as if he were going to force us off the road. Mike and I exchanged glances and viewed the situation with some trepidation. It was midnight in the desert, we were not sure who he was and we were visitors in a strange country. We decided to try and ignore him.

Looking out of the corner of my eye, I saw the driver swing the steering wheel over towards our car and I braked very hard just as the Mercedes cut across our nose, across the width of the carriageway and onto the verge. It started bouncing around on the edge of the road and we accelerated away as hard as possible in a 1300cc car, but it

wasn't long before the Mercedes was catching us again. The Arab came storming past and then locked all his brakes solid. By this time Mike and I were becoming very nervous about what was happening. The little Mitsubishi was only just able to outbrake the Mercedes and at the last minute I swung around it onto the verge. The driver tried to hold us there but we had enough speed to squeeze past and drove off towards Manama as quickly as our car would travel.

As we approached the outskirts of the capital the Mercedes was catching up again, but just as it drew alongside we darted down a slip road to take an alternative route. The Mercedes failed to stop at the junction and ploughed straight across the middle of the traffic island. We thought that this was the end of the pursuit but not so. We were about three or four miles up the next section when we saw the lights of the Mercedes following us up the wrong side of the motorway!

As the Armco ended the Mercedes swung across the reservation and continued its pursuit. We tucked in behind a small truck but the Mercedes came past and drove across both of us, taking the truck onto the verge. As the Arab came back off the banking he almost collected the side of us, and we desperately tried to accelerate away from him. While all this was going on, Mike was studying the maps and we were rapidly discussing where we could hide from this madman.

We decided that the first port of call would be the Radio Bahrain headquarters, where we had done an interview with local journalists the day before. As we arrived we saw that the building was in total darkness and opted for the Security Police Headquarters instead. We arrived in a big cloud of tyre smoke and were immediately surrounded at gunpoint by a number of soldiers. Eventually an English-speaking sergeant arrived and I explained that we were being pursued by a madman who had already forced two other vehicles off the road. At this

Opposite: in the desert with the Raid Paris–Dakar. The rally produced a striking juxtaposition of two cultures.

Right, Russell and Mike Broad celebrate victory on the Bahrain Rally; below, Russell attempts to thank the organizers (in Arabic!) for his successes on the event.

the situation very cleverly, guessing that the man had close connections with Britain because of his excellent English accent.

'You obviously live in England,' said Mike; 'Whereabouts?'

'I have a flat in Brighton,' replied the man.

'So you travel up the motorway to London. Would you stop for a hitchhiker on the M23?'

'Of course not,' he replied, and at that point I felt that he backed off. He talked to the soldiers in Arabic and then turned to us again: 'On this occasion I will forgive you and you may proceed,' he announced in a very off-hand manner. So we did eventually get back to Manama, but it was certainly one of the most alarming moments of my rallying career.

One of the most enjoyable events I ever tackled was the New Zealand Rally. Many people who have not been to the country imagine it to be like an England of thirty or forty years ago, but in fact it does have its own very special character. The people are very hospitable and it is one of the most interesting countries I have ever visited. I intend to take the family there in the future. I have never been to another place where there is such an enormous variety of scenery in a relatively small land area. In the far north you have tropical coral beaches with waving palm trees. One particularly spectacular sight is Ninety Mile Beach, which is exactly what the name suggests. A little further south on the east coast is the picturesque Bay of Islands, which is one of the most beautiful seascapes I have ever seen. Further south is an area of volcanic activity, mainly dedicated to sheep farming, with rolling hills. The east side of the North Island reminded me of Corsica, with its steep mountains and deep gorges, but undoubtedly the most impressive time for me was a stay at a hotel in Taupo, close to the town of Rotorua, where

moment my heart sunk, because as I was explaining our predicament to the sergeant, I spotted the Mercedes backing past the entrance to the Security Headquarters and driving into the slip road. As I was saying 'that's him, that's him', the Arab in question clambered out of his car and all the soldiers stood to attention and saluted him. He turned out to be the Commander-in-Chief of the National Guard!

At this moment we thought our lot was up. The man came across and, in perfect English, barked, 'Why didn't you stop when I signalled you to do so? You should always stop when someone waves you down.'

We explained that it was the middle of the night, we didn't know who it was and were generally unsure of the situation. He got very angry but Mike Broad then defused

Victory was sweet on the New Zealand Rally: Russell presses on through the forests near Rotorua.

The Andrews Escort flings the spray wide at a watersplash during the Castrol 75 Rally.

A page of pace notes for the infamous Abergwesyn–Tregaron road. Average speeds achieved over Welsh terrain like this made Russell doubt the wisdom of road rallying in its mid-1970s form.

Abergwesyn - Tregaron

Notes start Abergwesyn village

50 FL + FR FR 100 FR FR + FL + kink R +
(gate)
FL 50 FL 50 LFR + MR + FR crest
50 crest FL + FL 100 FR 50 FR
crest LFR 50 FR + crest + FR 50
crest FL 200 FR FL 50 crest FL!
200 to crest FL 50 FL + FR + crest FL
50 crest FR crest (small) 100 to dip
FL + FR + FL crest FL crest FR 50
bump + FL + LFR + FL + FR 50
F kink R + L FR + FML 200 (with kinks)
FR + crest BR !! 50 crest + ML ! Bridge
50 Bridge bumps ! + FL + LFR + ML
onto bridge FR + L crest crest + FR
FL + crest FR FR 100 climbing crest
50 HL 150 HR 50 FR + FL 50 FR + FL

there are numerous geysers and hot water springs.

Each bungalow in our particular motel was separated from others by a privet hedge, and under the shrubs were gushing hot-water springs and clouds of steam. At the door of each bungalow there was a green lawn leading to the shores of a beautiful blue lake. On the far side of Lake Taupo there are snow-covered alps used frequently for ski-ing and other winter sports. In the centre of the mountain range is a perfectly conical volcano, Mount Ngauruhoe, which, despite being covered in snow, is permanently belching steam and smoke, really quite an amazing sight.

Although the country is a similar size to Britain, the population is only in the region of four million people and, of those, one and a half million live in Auckland. This is one of the largest cities in the world in terms of geographical area. Most of the inhabitants live in houses with quarter-acre plots and because the city is spread out in this way it vies with Los Angeles for its size of sprawl.

I would dearly have loved to visit South Island, but the only view I had was across the Cook Straits. I understand the mountains are very beautiful there, with glaciers in the extreme south. From coral and palms to glaciers – it is hard to imagine such a small country having such a vast range of geographical experience to offer.

Shortly before the New Zealand Rally I went to visit my local doctor who has always been very helpful. I explained where I was going and that I was worried about jet-lag. He obtained five big sleeping pills for me on prescription and we worked out that I would do best not to travel via the regular route eastwards across Australia, but instead to take the Los Angeles western passage, which in itself was almost a ten-hour flight. This then left a twelve-hour trip to Auckland, one of the longest non-stop flights in the world at the time.

Two or three hours into the latter flight I took one of the 'big sleeping tablets' and promptly went out like a light. I was woken by the air stewardess as we arrived at Auckland at 07.00 on a New Zealand morning after a full nine hours unbroken sleep! That was the best cure I know for jet-lag.

Sleep, or rather the lack of it, reminds me of my road-rallying days and the one event which springs particularly to mind is the Targa Rusticana, John Brown's ultimate creation. It consisted of 270 competitive miles and even the petrol halts were in effect timed. These factors kept you on the go all night. I was extremely tired at the end of it and it was significant that so few competitors finished. This was the classic style of road rallying, but it was inevitable that a sport which was that competitive on public roads would have to come to an end.

In the same year, the problems were highlighted on the Gremlin Rally in central Wales. A six-week rule had been introduced to prevent roads being used for rallies twice within six weeks, but John Brown managed to get hold of some maps which had been used by another earlier rally in the same area and we were also aware of an event using the same patch a few weeks later. The number of roads available to the organizers was severely restricted, so we decided to make pace notes, over the three weekends prior to the rally, of the route we thought might be used. Much to our surprise we met Malcolm Patrick and Neil Wilson doing a similar thing, as well as Nigel Rockey and Paul White. Patrick drove a Porsche 911 and Rockey an RS1600.

We were competing in a Mexico and finished third behind this pair. But one thing shook me on this rally: there was one selective which started under the archway near the Myherin Forest stage above Devil's Bridge and wound its way through Cwmystwyth to the top of the Elan Valley dams and down the side of the Dams Road. At the end of the event we were talking to the Clerk of the Course and it would seem that on that section, in a standard Escort Mexico delivering a mere 90bhp, we'd averaged 72mph! It was at that point that we came to the conclusion that we shouldn't be doing this on open public roads. It was that event above all which made me feel that high-speed road rallying wasn't right under the circumstances, although I still believe that the future of British club rallying lies with a form of sport on the public roads, but with a navigational emphasis.

Road rallies always provided lots of excitement, none more than the Millimar, a round of the Mexico Championship. In a pea-souper fog we caught Cec Offley in his Marina, sedately following another competitor, who in turn was following what appeared in the fog to be a Mini van. John Brown screamed, 'I know this road. After the cattle grid it's open land – take them on the left!'

As we crossed the grid we set off on the grass and things became more and more hairy as we scrabbled past the cars. It became so bad that I wasn't able to take my eyes off the route ahead: had I done so I would have noticed that we were passing a police car! We slid on to the road ahead of him, but the policeman must have been so surprised that he didn't even take our number. He then stopped all the following rally cars and refused to let them pass until someone owned up as to who the 'madman' was. No one split on us, although they were all effectively put out of the rally by the time penalties incurred.

John Horton, who was working for Dunlop at the time, assisted Russell with pace notes during his outing on the Tulip Rally in 1978.

The next year we did the same rally, which used the same road, and again it was foggy. We caught an old Bedford van this time and John again shouted, 'You remember the road – take him on the right!'

As we came over the cattle grid we set off on the wet grass to pass the van. We swerved around the first obstacle, the back of the cattle grid warning sign, but the hedge cutters had been out and piled up an enormous mound of brambles. At 50mph the Mexico buried itself in the cuttings. It wouldn't reverse out and then we found that we couldn't open the doors either. I opened my window and the brambles reached in like monster's tentacles. Eventually we evacuated the car by kicking out the rear window. It was probably fate dealing us justice in the light of our antics the previous year!

John Brown's commitment on road rallies was something to behold. On one occasion, he had spotted that the fog was only above a certain height and so we took a much longer, but quicker, route using the main roads in the valleys. Nearing the junction where we were to rejoin the rally route, we saw that two cars were parked opposite each other leaving a gap about three inches narrower than a Mexico. As we came closer John realised that one of the cars was his own and the other belonged to a friend who was out spectating with John's wife. There was a definite waver in his voice as he cried 'Go for it!' and I crashed through the gap at 40mph!

Rallies with a special ingredient have not always been good ones, as I discovered when I tackled the Tulip Rally in 1978. The Tulip had always been one of the grand old names in rallying history, but this one certainly didn't live up to the legend. I hope the organizers aren't reading this, but, candidly, this event was the worst I have ever been on. The event was based near Rotterdam in Holland and, when we arrived, it readily became apparent that the regulations were eccentric to say the least, the most contentious point being that pace notes were permitted but practice was not. To ensure that these rules were adhered to, the organizers kept the route secret until four hours before the start of the rally. This gave all the local co-drivers an advantage because they had pace notes for all the stages from previous rallies: after four or five stages it became clear that we had serious problems.

It was then that Peter Bryant came up with a brilliant idea. Dunlop's John Horton was assisting us with the servicing arrangements at the time and we also borrowed a driver from Andrews Holland who didn't in fact speak much English. After I'd carefully briefed him on my system, John Horton and the Dutch driver set off to make pace notes of the stages in an estate car, because although the regulations stated that practice was not permitted by the driver or co-driver, they didn't say that other individuals couldn't make pace notes! John drove back over the stages a couple of times to check their accuracy, but the problem was how to relay the information to Peter and myself in time for us to use it to our advantage on the special stages. The rally was running roughly three hours behind John and if he hung around too long he would not be able to practice subsequent stages.

Peter Bryant equipped John with a large sheaf of envelopes and John hung around at each stage start until a group of marshals arrived to set up the stage. He then placed the pace notes in one of the envelopes, put Peter's name on the cover and implored the marshals to pass this urgent message on to the co-driver of car number four. In each case the unwitting marshal handed us the pace notes for the stage, Peter ripped open the envelope and off we went, setting fastest time after fastest time!

The rally ambled its way through Holland, southern Belgium and into Luxembourg, where there was only a rest halt because special-stage rallying is not permitted. It was quite clear that the Belgian organizers resented the intrusion of this Dutch rally and the available stages were definitely the dregs left over from good Belgian events. The event entered its third day as the route headed back through Belgium, but the organizers began to hit serious problems and the rally was running so late that competitors were in danger of arriving at stages after the period of the road-closing had expired.

They were unsure how to handle the situation and Peter Bryant came to the rescue. He rewrote page after page of the route book for them, leaving the organisers to reprint the new schedule and hand it out to the other competitors. Peter reviewed the situation after a couple more stages and rewrote the road book again for the organizers. We proceeded across the length of Belgium reading a road book entirely produced by Peter Bryant and based on the knowledge that he had gained through the first section of the rally. Without his assistance the event would have completely collapsed – but needless to say we only included those stages on which we knew we could do reasonably well!

This, we thought, was our way of seeking revenge on those who had used pace notes earlier in the event and we duly finished and won the Tulip Rally, which was a shadow of its former self. My disappointment was increased at the prize-giving when, instead of winning one of the coveted silver tulips that used to be handed out in times past, we were given a bunch of ordinary, horticultural tulips!

12

Rallying into the future

It is of course difficult to predict how the sport will progress in the future, but I firmly believe that rallying will pass through an exciting period between now and 1995, when the Group A regulations come to an end. The current situation is that four European manufacturers are being joined by five or six Japanese companies, all keen to contest both World and National rally championships. These firms will be investing large sums of money to advertise their successes and the high level of expenditure will also serve to promote the sport as a whole.

An added level of spectacle will be generated by the use of more powerful cars. Compared to their immediate predecessors – the Group B machines – Group A cars must at first have looked very dull and unexciting to the spectator. But as the horsepower figures have continued to increase to around the 400bhp mark, cars are once again becoming exciting to watch. On the other hand, however, if you give the sport a higher profile and attract more spectators, you also make it a bigger target. There are problems on the horizon which FISA, internationally, and the RAC MSA, nationally, must address. Those problems must be tackled successfully if rallying is to remain a major sport with a long-term future. There will be growing pressure from the green movement who are opposed to the motor car at the best of times and see the pinnacle of motoring activities as their prime target. As these groups gain more political sway, their fringe areas will be encouraged to become more active. Rallying must therefore project a responsible image in this context. This will be achieved by making enthusiasts more aware of their public image and, for example, by encouraging the use of lead-free fuel in rally cars. It might be worthwhile allowing only such cars on some rallies, amongst other measures. It would be interesting to introduce a diesel category into some events, although recent news suggests that diesel isn't as environmentally friendly as was once

thought. Such ideas can and should be explored, however.

The most important factor in overcoming potential objections, however, is to make rallying a more popular sport with an increasing number of regular followers and competitors. One only has to consider football and the traumas which that sport has gone through in recent years to appreciate the point. It is hard to imagine rallying being allowed to continue had more than thirty people been killed on a special stage. Yet that is what happened at the Heysel stadium in the 1980s, and there have been other deaths among spectators as well, but football survives because it is seen as a major national sport: the political consequences to any party which advocated that football be banned would be far-reaching indeed.

That indicates why we need to be strong in numbers, and highlights a situation which the RAC MSA in Great Britain needs to address as its first consideration. I believe that strength in numbers will be achieved not only by encouraging newcomers into the sport at the grass-roots level but also by making rallying more exciting at the top and thus generating more publicity. There is no doubt that it is the exciting and well publicized sport which brings in new members.

If you consider that 7,500 marshals are required to run the Lombard RAC Rally, it becomes evident how dependent we are on the average club competitor for the maintenance of rallying at the top level. For that reason too the policy of the RAC MSA should be aimed at recruiting people into the sport, because without these individuals the lifeblood of rallying is not maintained. A growth in numbers will both ensure a healthy sport and help protect it against environmentalists, and our cause will be that much stronger.

The President of the Swedish Automobile Club once told me that he had been given the brief to make motorsport more successful in his country. The standard by which they defined success was that he had to increase the number of competition licence holders by 50%. That is an ideal criterion and one which should be adopted in Britain: the performance of the RAC MSA could then be readily monitored. Every competitor and motor club member should be registered, even if they only compete in closed-to-club events, and issued with a low-cost limited licence. This would then give the RAC MSA direct access to everyone interested in the sport, and we would know how many people are actually involved in rallying. Without this definite information it is very difficult to convince outside organisations – governments, local authorities, pressure groups, media corporations – that we are a major sport with many participants involved in a pastime which should be taken seriously.

The governing body ought to initiate a long term campaign aimed at making the bottom levels of the sport more attractive. Specific measures should be taken to ensure that sufficient low-cost venues are available to allow special-stage rallies to take place on private land. At the same time, the RAC MSA should also encourage the running of suitable events on public roads, because no matter how many off-road venues are found they could never replace in full the facilities which are offered by the amazing network of narrow lanes in the United Kingdom. Educating club members to take part in low-speed navigational rallies would give more people a taste for the sport, be it as competitor, organizer or marshal.

When I first joined car clubs it was commonplace to hold small-scale events which involved autotests and production car trials in addition to a night navigational rally section. A large proportion of the club membership would take part in these motorsport functions. Maybe these weren't the most dramatic or competitive forms of rallying, but they provided a stimulus for members and an opportunity to develop the social aspect of the club. It is this area which I feel needs to be revitalized at a club level. Many motor clubs seem to have lost their way and are no longer the social centres they used to be. The RAC MSA should set up a small organization to encourage motor clubs to further social activities and become more interesting meeting places. I well remember the days of the Castrol motorsport quizzes which attracted such a lot of attention. There are many other ideas which the RAC MSA could support in terms of both advice and the provision of equipment.

What stops many new people coming into the sport is a combination of the cost and the complexity of producing a competition car. One of the great advantages of bringing acceptable rallying onto public roads is that club members could use their ordinary road vehicles and would not be involved in the expensive preparation and maintenance of a fully-fledged rally car. As soon as you progress to rallying on private land, the cars inevitably begin to become 'racing machines' and are not suitable for any other purpose. Over the years there has been an enormous proliferation of technical regulations, most of which are more or less unnecessary for the kind of event

envisaged. The RAC MSA should take steps to reduce and simplify these rules by weeding out the trivial ones. The guideline should be 'if in doubt, throw it out!' For high-speed rallying, the RAC MSA should simply adopt FISA vehicle regulations, which among other things would enable British competitors to tackle overseas rallies more easily.

In this country we have the tremendously valuable facility of being able to use Forestry Commission roads for our rallying. But this aspect has been perhaps over-emphasized in recent years so that people have ignored the fact that public roads are still available for competition use, so long as the events are of an acceptable nature. With the dramatic increase in Forestry Commission charges, people should now be directed to looking again at the use of public roads. Of course no one is suggesting a return to the excessive speeds of the old-style road rally championships, but properly organized events could become the mainstay of the sport, accessible to a much larger number of participants.

At the same time, it is also important that rallying is exciting and glamorous at the top. One should not worry about the cost aspect at the top level, because so long as the sport is exciting there will always be enough people financially able to compete. The RAC MSA should undertake a major campaign aimed at bringing rallying back to peak-time television, to make more people aware how exciting it can be and to attract leading overseas drivers to rounds of our top championships. Producers of television programmes are not fools. They have become aware that rallying has been in a period of stagnation over the last few years: no amount of money will persuade them to increase coverage until it is clear that the interest and excitement can be brought back. The current increase in the number of manufacturers taking part provides a potential opportunity to develop the image of the sport in this way. Rallying can be interesting to a wide public and there are ways to make it a high-profile glamour pastime. Such an image would be good for the future, because it is the high-profile sports which attract participants at the grass-roots level.

Also vital for the future is the continued availability of Forestry Commission roads. Ordinary club members perhaps rarely appreciate what an amazing asset that is, and the RAC MSA should go out of its way to protect it. The subject of closing public roads for motorsport has frequently been discussed, but it will never be possible in this country on a scale large enough to provide appropriate venues for rallying. If we were to gain orders to close suitable stretches of road, I can imagine the Forestry Commission being tempted to say that we no longer needed the forests, and our loss would then be far greater than our gain. Besides, if rallying used closed public roads the sport would be vulnerable to far greater pressure from residents' associations and environmentalists. It would ultimately be far more difficult to organize events, not least because of the cost of insuring against spectator injury.

Many British competitors look enviously towards Continental Europe where the majority of rallies take place on public roads. It should be appreciated that without that facility the sport would all but die in countries like France, Italy and Belgium. But as people become more and more protective of their own personal rights, and less tolerant of the activities of others, those events will face major difficulties. Already this has happened in several European countries, and even in Ireland it is becoming increasingly difficult to find suitable stretches of road for special-stage rallying.

In the United Kingdom we are insulated from that threat, because we have the use of Forestry Commission land. So long as rallying pays a more or less commercial

elsewhere there should be four overall directors for rallying, for racing, for karting and for other motorsports, operating under the umbrella of the chief executive but each having considerable autonomy to do the best for each branch of the sport.

For rallying to thrive, the RAC MSA requires an aggressive and innovative Director for Rallying. Whilst I disagree profoundly with many of the changes which FISA boss Jean-Marie Balestre has introduced, he has been a person prepared to stand up and be counted and willing, for better or worse, to make a definite decision one way or the other. I think that at, the end of the day, it is more valuable in the current climate to have someone like that at the helm, rather than a characterless

Russell talks about rallying, and the drizzle, to William Whitelaw (later Lord Whitelaw) on the occasion when the latter was invited to act as starter for the 1981 Tour of Cumbria Rally. It is important that politicians and others in positions of influence should understand the nature of the sport and appreciate that it has a considerable popular following.

charge for these facilities, the sport will continue. That is one of the reasons why Britain could be one of the last bastions in Europe of highly competitive motorsport.

At the heart of the problem is the structure of the RAC's motorsport division, with separate executives for Sporting Services, Technical Services, Marketing, Finance and Administration, nebulous titles which do not relate to the natural divisions of the sport or ensure accountability of the incumbent. This should be simplified so that each branch of the sport has its own director, responsible for its well-being. Their performance should be monitored, and I would suggest again that the increase in the number of participants in each area of the sport would be an excellent way of measuring progress. Obviously an executive for finance and administration is necessary, but

individual who may be technically well equipped but does not get things done. Balestre has done an enormous amount to promote motorsport and we need someone of that ilk at the RAC MSA.

A stumbling block in the past has been the reluctance of the RAC MSA to experiment or permit experimentation. The view seems to have been that a new idea once accepted will be perpetually enshrined, and that inhibits innovation in the first place. Far better to try an idea to see if it works, and throw it out the following year if it proves to be no good. For every five bad ideas, one will prove successful and the sport will benefit. It is worth remembering that in the late 1970s and early 1980s, when rallying was attracting far more interest, we went through a period of great experimentation in which new formats and new ideas were regularly tried out. Car regulations were in a state of flux and these changes attracted interest, not just among rally followers but also from sponsors and from the media.

The executives at the RAC MSA have very good ideas and are extremely capable in their function of administrating motorsport, but I feel that the organization needs to give them more freedom to carry out their projects. This would produce better results in the long term. I can't help feeling that someone like John Brown would have been the ideal candidate for the Director of

Much as the employees of the RAC MSA might not want to move premises again in the near future, I feel that one of the worst decisions they have taken in recent years was to move from Belgrave Square in London to a nondescript industrial estate at Colnbrook. I don't know the details of leases and costings, but, for all its inadequacies as a building, Belgrave Square was a prestigious address. A governing body should not be frightened to play on prestige: it is a factor to which both overseas visitors and people important to the sport in this country can relate.

Prior to the 1985 British Midland Ulster Rally, Russell discusses the politics of rallying with Linda Chalker, then Minister of Transport.

Rallying job. He probably wouldn't consider the position now, but at one time he was the perfect person. He speaks fluent French and Spanish, which would have been a great attribute when dealing with committees in Paris, he has always had the sporting interest at heart, he is very much in favour of the private entrant and he is not someone who would bow to pressure from lobbying. John is a colourful character and has a great ability to devise new ideas, which has been evident in his involvement in rallying over a number of years.

The RAC MSA needs to project a far better image to its customers. A small point, but one which highlights the way they don't do themselves any favours, is that it is impossible to get through the switchboard before 9.30 in the morning or between the hours of 12.00 and 2.00. If a commercial concern were to be run in this manner it would swiftly be out of business.

If it was not possible to maintain offices at such an address in Central London, the RAC MSA should have taken a much bolder step and moved to a geographically central location in England where they would have been accessible to ordinary motor club members. An ideal site would have been in the Midlands, close to Birmingham International Airport, the National Exhibition Centre and the hub of the rail network.

In summary, I feel that for the next four or five years rallying has a very rosy future, but it may well run into major problems after that. In a world where people seem to be shouting and thumping the table for their own ends, the governing body of motorsport needs to make sure that it is heard amongst those who could determine our future, and needs to be seen to be protecting our heritage. For the future good of the sport, we need an organization which is prepared to stand up and be counted.

RESULTS, 1969–1990

1969

EVENT	STATUS	CAR	RESULT
Welsh	International	Mini 850	1st in class
Scottish	International	Mini 850	3rd in class
RAC	International	Mini 850	2nd in class
Empire Trophy	Restricted	Mini 850	1st in class, 10th o/a

1970

EVENT	STATUS	CAR	RESULT
Welsh	International	Mini 998 Gp1	1st in class, 18th o/a
Sherry	International	Mini 1275 S Gp1	1st in class, 10th o/a

1971

EVENT	STATUS	CAR	RESULT
Dubonnet	Restricted	Mini 1275 Gp2	8th
Welsh Marches	Restricted	Mini 1275 Gp2	5th
Nutcracker	Restricted	Mini 1275 Gp2	4th
Gremlin	Restricted	Mini 1275 Gp2	3rd
Sherry	International	Mini 1275 Gp2	1st in class, 7th o/a

1972

EVENT	STATUS	CAR	RESULT
Scottish	International	Mini 998 Gp1	1st in class, 25th o/a
Sherry	International	Mini 1275 Gp2	1st in class, 6th o/a
Moss Tyres	Restricted	Ford Escort Mexico	2nd in class, 6th o/a
Bristowe	Restricted	Ford Escort Mexico	4th in class, 7th o/a
Hereford Evening News	Restricted	Ford Escort Mexico	5th in class, 6th o/a
Cytax	Restricted	Ford Escort Mexico	4th
Peak Revs	Restricted	Ford Escort Mexico	4th
Gremlin	Restricted	Ford Escort Mexico	10th
Eastwood	Restricted	Ford Escort Mexico	7th
Torbay	Restricted	Ford Escort Mexico	2nd in class, 3rd o/a
Taunton	Restricted	Ford Escort Mexico	1st
Virgo Galaxy	Restricted	Ford Escort Mexico	1st
Tour of Epynt	Restricted	Ford Escort Mexico	1st in class, 4th o/a

Castrol/*Motoring News* Championship			10th
Ford Mexico Championship			4th

1973

EVENT	STATUS	CAR	RESULT
Jim Clark	National	Ford Escort RS1600	2nd in class, 2nd o/a
Border	National	Ford Escort Mexico	1st in class, 3rd o/a
Targa Rusticana	Restricted	Ford Escort Mexico	1st
Mini Miglia	Restricted	Ford Escort Mexico	6th
Red Dragon	Restricted	Ford Escort Mexico	1st in class, 2nd o/a
Bristowe	Restricted	Ford Escort Mexico	2nd in class, 2nd o/a
Welsh Marches	Restricted	Ford Escort Mexico	2nd in class, 2nd o/a
Border 200	Restricted	Ford Escort Mexico	1st in class, 2nd o/a
Hereford Evening News	Restricted	Ford Escort Mexico	1st
Wye	Restricted	Ford Escort Mexico	1st
Eagle	Restricted	Ford Escort Mexico	1st
Nutcracker	Restricted	Ford Escort Mexico	1st in class, 3rd o/a
CSMA	Restricted	Ford Escort Mexico	1st in class, 2nd o/a
Gremlin	Restricted	Ford Escort Mexico	1st in class, 2nd o/a
Gwynedd	Restricted	Ford Escort Mexico	1st
Stocktonian	Restricted	Ford Escort Mexico	9th

EVENT	STATUS	CAR	RESULT
Cilwendeg	Restricted	Ford Escort Mexico	1st in class, 2nd o/a
Britvic	Restricted	Ford Escort Mexico	1st
Plains	Restricted	Ford Escort Mexico	1st
Taunton	Restricted	Ford Escort Mexico	1st in class, 2nd o/a
Chieftan	Restricted	Ford Escort Mexico	1st in class, 5th o/a

Welsh Rally Championship			1st
Castrol/*Motoring News* Championship			2nd
Ford/*Daily Express* Championship			2nd

1974

EVENT	STATUS	CAR	RESULT
Boucles de Spa	International	Ford Escort Mexico	1st in class, 6th o/a
Circuit of Ireland	International	Ford Escort Mexico	3rd in class, 13th o/a
Welsh	International	Opel Ascona 1.9S	4th in class, 20th o/a
Donegal	International	Ford Escort RS2000	1st in class, 8th o/a
Avon Tour of Britain	International	Ford Escort RS2000	11th
Manx Trophy	International	Ford Escort RS2000	1st in class, 9th o/a
Larne Texaco	National	Ford Escort RS2000	1st in class, 6th o/a
Jim Clark	National	Ford Escort RS2000	2nd in class, 7th o/a
Castrol 75	National	Ford Escort RS2000	1st in class, 2nd o/a
Dukeries	National	Ford Escort RS2000	1st in class, 12th o/a
Lindisfarne	National	Ford Escort RS2000	3rd in class, 9th o/a
Tour of Lincs	Restricted	Ford Escort RS2000	2nd in class
Mintex Dales	Restricted	Ford Escort RS2000	1st in class, 14th o/a
Cheltenham Festival	Restricted	Ford Escort RS2000	6th in class

Castrol/*Autosport* Group 1 Rally Championship			1st
RAC Group 1 Rally Championship			2nd
Castrol/*Autosport* Rally Championship			5th
RAC Rally Championship			11th

1975

EVENT	STATUS	CAR	RESULT
Mintex	International	Ford Escort RS2000	1st in Gp1, 8th o/a
Circuit of Ireland	International	Ford Escort RS2000	1st in Gp1, 5th o/a
Welsh	International	Ford Escort RS1800	5th
Scottish	International	Ford Escort RS1800	2nd
Granite City	National	Ford Escort RS1600	5th
Avon Tour of Britain	National	Ford Escort RS2000	6th
Burmah	National	Ford Escort RS1800	2nd

European Rally Championship			15th
RAC Rally Championship			4th
Castrol/*Autosport* Rally Championship			7th

1976

EVENT	STATUS	CAR	RESULT
Mintex	International	Ford Escort RS1800	2nd
Circuit of Ireland	International	Ford Escort RS1800	2nd
Scottish	International	Ford Escort RS1800	1st
Tour of Dean	National	Ford Escort RS1800	3rd
Granite City	National	Ford Escort RS1800	1st
Jim Clark	National	Ford Escort RS1800	2nd
Burmah	National	Ford Escort RS1800	3rd
Castrol	National	Ford Escort RS1800	1st

RAC Rally Championship			2nd
European Rally Championship			10th
Castrol/*Autosport* Rally Championship			5th

1977

EVENT	STATUS	CAR	RESULT
Circuit of Ireland	International	Ford Escort RS1800	1st
Tulip	International	Ford Escort RS1800	3rd
Scottish	International	Ford Escort RS1800	3rd
Granite City	National	Ford Escort RS1800	1st
Jim Clark	National	Ford Escort RS1800	1st
Castrol	National	Ford Escort RS1800	2nd
Burmah	National	Ford Escort RS1800	2nd
Ulster	National	Ford Escort RS1800	2nd
RAC	International	Ford Escort RS1800	3rd

European Rally Championship			4th
RAC Open Rally Championship			1st

1978

EVENT	STATUS	CAR	RESULT
Burmah	International	Ford Escort RS1800	1st =
New Zealand	International	Ford Escort RS1800	1st
Circuit of Ireland	International	Ford Escort RS1800	1st
Rallysprint	International	Ford Escort RS1800	3rd
Tulip	International	Ford Escort RS1800	1st
Mintex	International	Ford Escort RS1800	2nd
Welsh	International	Ford Escort RS1800	5th
Scottish	International	Ford Escort RS1800	7th
Donington Rallysprint	International	Ford Escort RS1800	2nd
RAC	International	Ford Escort RS1800	3rd

European Rally Championship			9th
RAC Open Rally Championship			2nd

1979

EVENT	STATUS	CAR	RESULT
Mintex	International	Ford Escort RS1800	4th
Welsh	International	Ford Escort RS1800	2nd
Scottish	International	Ford Escort RS1800	10th
Rallysprint	International	Ford Escort RS1800	3rd
Manx	International	Ford Escort RS1800	1st
RAC	International	Ford Escort RS1800	2nd
Phillipines	International	Ford Escort RS2000	2nd

RAC Open Rally Championship			2nd

1980

EVENT	STATUS	CAR	RESULT
Gwynedd	National	Talbot Sunbeam Lotus	4th
Welsh	International	Talbot Sunbeam Lotus	3rd
RAC	International	Talbot Sunbeam Lotus	4th

RAC Open Rally Championship			11th

1981

EVENT	STATUS	CAR	RESULT
Mintex	International	Talbot Sunbeam Lotus	5th
Circuit of Ireland	International	Talbot Sunbeam Lotus	3rd
Rallysprint	International	Talbot Sunbeam Lotus	3rd
Gwynedd	National	Talbot Sunbeam Lotus	1st
Rallysprint	International	Talbot Sunbeam Lotus	6th
Tour of Cumbria	National	Talbot Sunbeam Lotus	1st
Pace	National	Talbot Sunbeam Lotus	2nd

EVENT	STATUS	CAR	RESULT
Rallysprint	National	Talbot Sunbeam Lotus	1st
RAC Open Rally Championship			5th

1982

EVENT	STATUS	CAR	RESULT
Wyedean	National	Vauxhall Chevette HSR	1st
Mintex	International	Vauxhall Chevette HSR	6th
West Cork	International	Vauxhall Chevette HSR	1st
Circuit of Ireland	International	Vauxhall Chevette HSR	2nd
Rallysprint	International	Vauxhall Chevette HSR	2nd
Rallysprint	International	Vauxhall Chevette HSR	2nd
Haspengouw	International	Vauxhall Chevette HSR	2nd
Scottish	International	Vauxhall Chevette HSR	4th
Hunsruck	International	Vauxhall Chevette HSR	3rd
1,000 Lakes	International	Vauxhall Chevette HSR	6th
Manx	International	Vauxhall Chevette HSR	2nd
Peter Russek	National	Vauxhall Chevette HSR	5th
Pace	National	Vauxhall Chevette HSR	2nd
RAC	International	Vauxhall Chevette HSR	6th
RAC Open Rally Championship			4th
European Rally Championship			11th
West Euro Cup			3rd
Irish Tarmac Rally Championship			2nd

1983

EVENT	STATUS	CAR	RESULT
Mintex	International	Vauxhall Chevette HSR	4th
Circuit of Ireland	International	Vauxhall Chevette HSR	1st
Welsh	International	Vauxhall Chevette HSR	2nd
Scottish	International	Vauxhall Chevette HSR	3rd
Ulster	International	Vauxhall Chevette HSR	3rd
Manx	International	Vauxhall Chevette HSR	3rd
Audi Sport	National	Vauxhall Chevette HSR	2nd
RAC	International	Vauxhall Chevette HSR	5th
RAC Open Rally Championship			2nd
Irish Tarmac Rally Championship			2nd

1984

EVENT	STATUS	CAR	RESULT
Wyedean	National	Opel Manta 400	1st
National Breakdown	International	Opel Manta 400	3rd
Welsh	International	Opel Manta 400	2nd
Scottish	International	Opel Manta 400	3rd
Ulster	International	Opel Manta 400	2nd
Cyprus	International	Opel Manta 400	2nd
RAC	International	Opel Manta 400	4th
Bahrain	International	Talbot Sunbeam Lotus	1st
RAC Open Rally Championship			3rd

1985

EVENT	STATUS	CAR	EVENT
National Breakdown	International	Opel Manta 400	2nd
Circuit of Ireland	International	Opel Manta 400	2nd
Scottish	International	Opel Manta 400	3rd
Hunsruck	International	Opel Manta 400	5th
Ulster	International	Opel Manta 400	1st

EVENT	STATUS	CAR	RESULT
Manx	International	Opel Manta 400	1st
Cyprus	International	Opel Manta 400	3rd
RAC	International	Opel Manta 400	8th
RAC Open Rally Championship			1st

1986

EVENT	STATUS	CAR	RESULT
National Breakdown	International	Opel Manta 400	4th
Circuit of Ireland	International	Opel Manta 400	2nd
Welsh	International	Opel Manta 400	4th
Scottish	International	Opel Manta 400	5th
Ulster	International	Opel Manta 400	5th
Manx	International	Opel Manta 400	5th
RAC Open Rally Championship			2nd

1987

EVENT	STATUS	CAR	RESULT
National Breakdown	International	Opel Manta 400	2nd
Manx National	National	Vauxhall Astra GTE	5th
Welsh	International	Opel Manta 400	1st
Kayel Graphics	National	Vauxhall Astra GTE	1st in GpA, 4th o/a
Scottish	International	Vauxhall Astra GTE	7th
Cumbria	National	Vauxhall Astra GTE	2nd in GpA
Manx	International	Vauxhall Astra GTE	5th
Quip	National	Vauxhall Astra GTE	2nd in GpA, 10th o/a
Audi Sport	National	Vauxhall Astra GTE	2nd in GpA, 9th o/a
Truck Grand Prix	International	Renault	2nd up-to-300bhp final
Marlboro National Rally Championship			2nd

1988

EVENT	STATUS	CAR	RESULT
Scottish	International	Ford Sierra Cosworth	3rd
24 Hours of Ypres	International	Ford Sierra Cosworth	5th
Audi Sport	National	Ford Sierra Cosworth	1st

1989

EVENT	STATUS	CAR	RESULT
Cartel	International	Ford Sierra Cosworth	3rd
Circuit of Ireland	International	Ford Sierra Cosworth	2nd
Welsh	International	Ford Sierra Cosworth	2nd
Scottish	International	Ford Sierra Cosworth	4th
Ulster	International	Ford Sierra Cosworth	2nd
Manx	International	Ford Sierra Cosworth	1st
Audi Sport	International	Ford Sierra Cosworth	8th
Rally of the Lakes	International	Ford Sierra Cosworth	1st
RAC Open Rally Championship			2nd
Irish Tarmac Rally Championship			1st

1990

EVENT	STATUS	CAR	RESULT
Cartel	International	Ford Sierra 2.9i 4x4	4th
Scottish	International	Ford Sierra 2.9i 4x4	3rd
Manx	International	Ford Sierra Cosworth 4x4	1st
Audi Sport	International	Ford Sierra Cosworth 4x4	1st
RAC	International	Ford Sierra Cosworth 4x4	36th